LOST HOUSES
IN
NANTWICH

ANDREW LAMBERTON AND ROBIN GRAY

Published by

Landmark Publishing Ltd
Ashbourne Hall, Cokayne Ave, Ashbourne, Derbyshire DE6 1EJ England
Tel: (01335) 347349 Fax: (01335) 347303
e-mail: landmark@clara.net
website: www.landmarkpublishing.co.uk

ISBN 1 84306 202 X

© Andrew Lamberton & Robin Gray 2005

Dedication
This book is dedicated to the memory of Dorothy Vaughan whose deep affection for
Nantwich and its history has been an inspiration.

Print: Cromwell Press Ltd, Trowbridge
Design: Mark Titterton
Cover: James Allsopp

Front cover: Birchen House.
Title page: Black and White Houses in Welsh Row.
Back cover top: Whitehall, Welsh Row.
Back cover bottom left: Black and White Houses in Welsh Row.
Back cover bottom right: Painting of The Old Gaol House.

LANDMARK COLLECTOR'S LIBRARY

Lost Houses
in
Nantwich

Andrew Lamberton and Robin Gray

Landmark Publishing

ACKNOWLEDGEMENTS

We would particularly like to thank Judy St. Pourcain and Peter Clough who have helped with research, providing personal reminiscences and photographs, to Melvyn Reynolds for his expertise in producing the maps and Kevin Greener in the computer transfer of all the many illustrations to disc.

We would like to thank Nantwich Museum Board of Trustees who allowed us to use some of the photographs from the museum collection, and also Mike Eddison, Local Studies Adviser, for permission to use some illustrations from the County Record Office at Chester.

Thanks are also due to Allan Whatley for his advice and guidance on writing skills; we are also grateful to Nancy Dutton, Reg and Barbara Baker, Rosemarie Corfield and Janet Gray, all of whom provided personal reminiscences and photographs; Also to the following who provided photographs for inclusion, Gwen Thompson, Anne Copeland, Olive Williams, Harry Clewlow, John Brough, Rev. Peter Chantry, Doreen Thomas and Tony and Margaret Graham; to Peter Wall for permission to use information and photographs on AN Hornby; to Mr P Murphy for providing details on the Cedars, Marsh Lane; thanks are also due to the information sources at Nantwich Library, *Nantwich Chronicle*, Cheshire Record Office and Keele University; to Pauline Crump of Peter Williams, Chemist, for assistance with photograph reproduction, and Mark and Julie Simon of The Paper Place for copying facilities.

CONTENTS

INTRODUCTION

Recent rapid growth in our environment has reminded us that many houses in Nantwich have gone forever and it was thought that now was the time to document these buildings while still within living memory.

A definition of lost houses includes those that are no longer with us or have changed so dramatically in appearance as to be virtually unrecognisable from the original.

It was decided to include all types of house from the large homes of the well-to-do such as Townsend House, Whitehall and Elm House, to the many small cottages of the poorer population. Indeed, Nantwich owes much of its attraction to the juxtaposition of these houses with each other. Not only do we have a difference in size but also a wide variation in building styles from black and white Elizabethan through elegant Georgian to the brick and slate Victorian architecture, and standing next to each other. Together, they provide a unique, and nowadays quite rare, vision of a market town not swamped by high street chain stores that can be seen in most towns today. Emphasis has been placed on domestic buildings and where possible information has been sought to find out who lived there.

Houses lost during the 1583 Fire of Nantwich have been comprehensively covered by Eric Garton and Jeremy Lake in their respective publications and therefore have not been included (apart from the odd exception) in this book.

Victorian directories have proved particularly useful but it is interesting to note that the poorer areas such as the Wood Streets and Snowhill were not included in the street inhabitants' lists. *Johnson's Almanacs* have been indispensable, and the writings of William Willett, Rupert Bell and Harry Johnson, invaluable in giving us an insight into the many characters who were well-known in Nantwich over one hundred years ago.

Some public buildings have also been included as they had an important role in the community in the past. The Market Hall, and the old Town Hall particularly spring to mind. The old Grammar School was another such important building, what a great shame that it was demolished. Many religious buildings have now disappeared with the decline and changes in worship and these include Baptist, Methodist and Unitarian Chapels. The Brine Baths Hotel had to be an obvious inclusion but equally important was Parkfield, the home of Albert Hornby the famous cricketer. Manufacturing establishments such as clothing factories and tanneries have also been given some attention.

Each individual property (or sometimes group of properties) has been allocated a number, which is used to aid the reader in identifying its exact location in the accompanying maps. Where it has been impossible to identify an exact location the buildings have been placed at the end of the street section and its corresponding number will not be found on the map.

The maps are based on the Ordnance Survey 3rd Edition of 1910. Old watercourses, such as the Frog Channel in Welsh Row and the Lothburn Drain between Churchyardside and Beam Street have been inserted, as have streets not built in 1910, such as Queen's Drive and Manor Road.

Many photographs and pictures have also been included to help illustrate the text, most of them having not been previously published.

The reasons for demolition are often unclear, some which were documented had previously suffered a serious fire and were not thought worth saving, while the majority were probably in such a poor state that it was necessary to demolish. Some were immediately replaced with another building on the same site, others making way for several properties to be built there.

In the first section of the book, the reader is taken on a journey through the main streets of the town, starting from the west end of Welsh Row and moving in an easterly direction finishing at the eastern end of Hospital Street, covering eight main streets.

The second section covers the town outskirts, starting in the north on the Barony and then moving in a clockwise direction finally finishing in Marsh Lane to the south-west. This section includes some of the grander houses of the more well-to-do as well as outlying farms.

Every effort has been made to locate individual properties accurately using local maps and street directories; however it must be appreciated that the task becomes increasingly difficult the further back in time that one goes. A numbering system for houses in Nantwich streets was not introduced until the mid 1870s.

The present street numbering system has been used for this book and it needs to be mentioned that some numbers have been altered since they were introduced, particularly the far end of Hospital Street, London Road and Crewe Road.

We have tried to be as exhaustive as possible, but inevitably there may well be buildings that have for one reason or another been overlooked. For this, we apologise in advance. I would be grateful to hear from any reader who can add to the list.

Section 1

NANTWICH TOWN

Welsh Row

1 The Toll House
2 Cottage Hospital
3 Sir Roger Wilbraham s almhouses
4 St.Lawrence s Hospital
5 The Tannery
6 111-123 Welsh Row
7 York Buildings
8 Townsend House
9 75-77 Welsh Row
10 Kingsley Fields
11 White Hall
12 35-37 Welsh Row
13 Middle Stych
14 Gas Works
15 34-40 Welsh Row
16 Wood Streets
17 19 Welsh Row
18 2-4 Welsh Row

Diagram based on the Ordnance Survey 25in map of 1910

1 Welsh Row

1. The Toll House

At the western end of Welsh Row, at the end of Welshman's Lane stood a tollhouse for the Nantwich to Chester Turnpike Road. In 1861 William Welch aged 37 lived here. He worked as a labourer on the turnpike road while his wife Ann collected the tolls. Due mainly to the impact of the railway, turnpikes lost their status and custom, soon falling into rapid decline. Finally the tollhouse was demolished around 1875 along with three others around the town. Harry Johnson, printer, publisher of *Johnson's Almanacs* and local historian, in his reminiscences written in the 1953 edition, remembers the tollgate still hanging here at the side of the road.

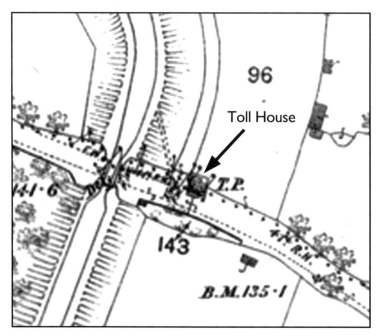

Welsh Roe Toll House.

2. The Cottage Hospital

The Cottage Hospital was built in 1911, from voluntary contributions in the community, to provide treatment that could not be efficiently undertaken at home. It was maintained also by subscriptions, donations and fund-raising events such as the annual Cottage Hospital fête. It continued to provide an invaluable service to the local community for another 60 years but was eventually closed following the opening of the large area hospital at Leighton near Crewe. The building was used for other purposes for a number of years but was eventually demolished in 1999 to make way for a housing development.

Nantwich Cottage Hospital. Built with donations and private subscriptions.

3. Sir Roger Wilbraham's Almshouses

Nearer to the town stand the Tollemache Almshouses, built on the gardens of the original Sir Roger Wilbraham's Almshouses. These were of a single storey, brick building divided into six to accommodate four poor almsmen from Nantwich and two from Acton parish. Each almsman had his own individual garden behind the building which stood close to the highway, having a wall in front with a gateway in the middle. It is believed that the original stone gateway was transferred a long time ago to the garden of Townsend House further along Welsh Row towards the town. This gateway was later purchased by William Spencer Tollemache, a descendant of Sir Roger Wilbraham, and installed in the grounds of Dorfold Hall where it can still be seen today. In the centre of the almshouses was a stone tablet of the Wilbraham coat of arms dated 1613.

As well as free accommodation, every two years each almsman was provided with a warm coat of grey cloth faced with blue and a cap. Every year they were given a pair of shoes and forty shillings. In 1646, John Pratchett, a poor almsman was paid two shillings for the rent of his almshouse to be used as a sentry or guard house for the Nantwich garrison.

The Almshouses were rebuilt by Lord John Tollemache in 1870 on the gardens behind the original building in two groups of three, and are two storeys high. They were renamed the Tollemache Almshouses and were modernised in 1986.

Sir Roger Wilbraham also had almshouses built for two poor almsmen in Acton Churchyard in the same year, and these are still in existence. These will no doubt be very similar if not identical to the Nantwich Almshouses. What is very noticeable at Acton is the lack of space and any modern amenities, for example water, sanitation etc.

4. St. Lawrence's Hospital

Of even earlier foundation was St. Lawrence's Hospital, a 'lazar' house or hospital for lepers, according to town tradition to have been situated on or near the malthouse immediately adjacent to the almshouses. An Inquisition in 1354 refers to the Abbey of Combermere possessing the hospital in which:

'there ought to be a chaplain to sing divine service daily and in which there ought to be three beds for the reception of poor sick people where they shall remain until they have recovered health.'

Very little is known about this hospital but it is thought that bathing in brine was a recommended treatment for leprosy. The hospital appears to have closed around 1548 and the last incumbent was Richard Wright receiving an annual pension of £3.8s.4d as late as 1562. He seems to have purchased the associated lands as in his Inquisition post mortem of 1589 he is said to have died owning a pasture called Chapel Croft, half of another pasture called Chapel Field adjacent, lying in Acton and the tithes of the formerly dissolved free chapel of St. Lawrence.

The Rev. Joseph Partridge in his *History of Nantwich* printed in 1774 refers to a priory also in existence 'Over and against the almshouses' and partly on the malthouse site. The building was still standing in 1653 because it is mentioned in an agreement in the Wilbraham manuscripts. It says that:

'Whereas the said John Thrush being lawfully possessed of a messuage called the Hospitall now divided into three dwellings in/near the Welsh Row in Wich Malbanke and one pasture/croft called the Hospitall croft in Wich Malbanke etc.'

There is a suggestion that No.155 Welsh Row, immediately opposite could be the Priory site. The malthouse, occupied by James Bayley in 1774, stood immediately behind what is now malthouse cottage and was still standing although empty around 1880, when James Hall was writing his *History of Nantwich*.

5. The Tannery

Immediately opposite the almshouses stood the tannery, consisting of a tan house, engine house (presently still standing but dilapidated) and tan pits. The pits would hold lime at various strengths and ground oak bark, again at different strengths. The Tannery was extremely busy in the 1850s, providing leather for the local shoe trade, with the tan pits a hive of industry and large stacks of oak bark everywhere. Apparently the putrid smell coming from the hides soaking in tan pits was particularly obnoxious and unpleasant.

It is thought that William Jackson may have built a tannery here in 1655 and he is mentioned again in the 1691 Nantwich Rate Book with a house and tan house. The tannery came into the ownership of James Tomkinson in 1792 and was occupied by George and Thomas Taylor. It became the business premises of King Nixon in 1834, then Thomas Nixon, then William Cooper in 1874, Shackerley, Boston and Co. in 1892 and afterwards, W. Blud, fellmonger (dealer in hides), only ceasing production as a small skin preparation business in 2002 after a further change of ownership.

6. 111–123 Welsh Row

Moving further along Welsh Row towards the town centre, just after Marsh Lane end, two modern houses set back from the road mark the position of a row of seven cottages fronting onto Welsh Row. The five nearest Marsh Lane were black and white with, at one time, thatched roofs, the other two being brick-built. There was no pavement in 1851 and the three cottages nearest the town centre each had a step up to the front door which jutted out into the street.

Old black and white cottages in Welsh Row near Marsh Lane end. The roofs were originally thatched.

7. York Buildings

The Primitive Methodist Chapel in Welsh Row marks the site of York Buildings, erected in 1780 on land provided by George Wilbraham of Townsend. These consisted of four parallel rows of wooden shops or stalls and were used by travelling cloth merchants at the Cloth Fair, the Great Fair and the Christmas Rag Fair.

Rents collected from the merchants on 4 September 1783 at the third annual Cloth Fair amounted to £34. 15s. 9d. The 1792 map of Nantwich by Joseph Fenna shows the four rows of shops quite clearly.

8. Townsend House

Directly opposite the Methodist Chapel, on what is now King's Court, stood Townsend House, the garden of which was later built on by the Cheshire Constabulary for a Police Station and Courts.

The building of Townsend House by Richard Wilbraham began in 1575 and he moved into the completed house on the 6 August 1580. On the 25 August 1617, King James stayed a night at Townsend on his way back to London from Scotland. The following day he attended a service at the church, listening to a sermon by Dr Thomas Dodd, and then walked to the brine pit to see how the brine was fetched up in leather buckets from the well and poured

Townsend House. Originally built by the Wilbraham family, it was one of the major buildings in the town and converted later to a brewery, a clothing factory and finally a private house.

into wooden troughs that took it to the wich houses. In the afternoon, he left after dinner at Townsend to travel to Gerard's Bromley in Staffordshire.

Townsend House continued in the possession of the Wilbraham family until around 1780 when the family moved to a new mansion at Delamere. Dr Ormerod refers to the remains of the house in 1819 as having been lofty and spacious, with large bay windows surrounded by numerous outbuildings of timber and plaster, the gardens having high brick walls, stone ornaments of armorial bearings and grotesque devices.

The house was converted into a brewery and sold to Messrs Brooke and Quane prior to 1824. In 1825, the brewery was the venue for the first meeting of the Nantwich Auxiliary of the Bible Society.

A rare pottery jug made by Enoch Wood and dated 1818, showing the Townsend Brewery on both sides, was sold in 1990 for a record sum. On one side the view is of Namptwich Brewery showing a walled yard and three buildings all with smoking chimneys. The reverse shows a similar view but without the front wall and men

A rare Enoch Wood ceramic jug dated 1818 showing the earliest illustration of Townsend as Namptwich Brewery.

loading a dray with barrels using a winch pulley. One barrel is marked 'Double Strong' and another 'Harold Knight 1818'. Beeston Castle is visible on a far hilltop.

The brewery was later sold to Thomas Kirkbride, brewer. A billhead shows that Quane and Kirkbride were in partnership in 1831. Mr Kirkbride became the sole owner afterwards and then later he sold the buildings to George Harlock, a Quaker, who converted it into a clothing factory, part of which became a private house for the owner. The clothing produced initially at the factory was moleskin, corduroy and fustian, but later, around the 1860s, it was used to produce clothes for ordinary working people. The factory was a major employer in the town.

In 1906 it was the Nantwich Co-operative Boot and Shoe Factory. More recently the building was converted into a private house. This eventually became the residence of the late AO Bevan, a solicitor in the town, and after his death around 1964, the house was demolished and the site occupied by a petrol station and garage. These have since been demolished and King's Court is now situated on this site.

A row of ten cottages immediately behind Townsend House in King's Lane has also been demolished. Olive Halligan remembers living in one of them and describes them.

'Two of the cottages in the terrace were two-storey, the other eight were three-storey. In the two-storeyed houses, the front door opened straight into a square living room. The kitchen was at the back in which were the stairs. There was only cold water and the only toilet was at the bottom of the garden.

In the three-storeyed houses, again there was no hallway, the front door opening

into the living room but this time, a door in the corner of the living room led to the stairs. There was a black-leaded grate with an oven and a large cupboard on one side of the fireplace. The kitchen was at the back and again there was only cold water but there was a boiler built in the corner for washing clothes. The back door opened onto a shared yard and a toilet at the bottom of the garden. There was gas lighting.'

Gateway in the gardens of Dorfold Hall, Acton. This was thought to have originated outside the Wilbraham almshouses at the end of Welsh Row, then moved to Townsend House and finally to Dorfold Hall.

9. 75,77 Welsh Row

The entrance to Queen's Drive from Welsh Row marks the spot where two houses were demolished in the mid-1950s to make way for a new housing estate behind.

One of these houses was an almshouse founded by Roger Wilbraham in 1705 and intended for two old maids from the town. It was a small house consisting of two rooms, one up and one down, with one fireplace, a cold water tap and an earth closet in the yard. With no back entrance, coal deliveries and night-soil collection had to pass through the house. Walter Willett, a former Nantwich man refers to the latter in his reminiscences of old Nantwich printed in the *Nantwich Chronicle* in 1938. After 9 o'clock on a Friday night, every week throughout the year, the night-soil cart, an iron horse-drawn vessel, could be heard rumbling through the cobbled streets. Two men would enter the house, walk through to the rear and carry the pail back through the house, emptying it into the cart and returning with the empty pail. The awful accompanying obnoxious smell can be imagined!

In 1860, the inmates received 15s. each per quarter from Mr Wilbraham's agent, 3s. 4d. each for coals, a dress every other year and once per year, £2. 1s. from William Sprout's Bequest.

Census Returns from 1841 through to 1881, refer to only one almswoman in the property. There was also only a single occupant in 1939. Just a year later the house was sold to the local authority with a view to eventual demolition.

10. Kingsley Fields

At Red Lion Lane, next to the Wilbraham Arms, is the entrance to Kingsley Fields. The Wilbraham Arms was originally called the Red Lion, hence the name of the Lane. The fields were named after John Kingsley, a local man who came to live here around 1400 and owned a considerable amount of property and land. It is thought that he may have lived on the site of Porch House, immediately in front of the fields. Kingsley Fields were used as a cricket ground by Nantwich Cricket Club from the mid-1800s until they moved to the Barony Park around 1957. The famous England and Lancashire batsman A N Hornby, who lived in the town, played for the Nantwich team here on many occasions.

Kingsley Cottage. Previously called Kingsley Nursery. This may have been an early barn conversion.

On the right of Red Lion Lane is Kingsley Farm, the last working farm within the town boundary. This has now ceased operation as a farm.

At the end of the Lane on the right stood Kingsley Nursery. This building may have originally been a barn or outhouse belonging to Kingsley Farm and then later converted into a dwelling. In 1875 there was an extensive nursery behind the property. The occupier was Henry Plant, nurseryman, seedsman and florist who had a shop in High Street. In 1939, George Taylor, market gardener, nurseryman and dairy farmer lived here. The building was demolished in 2003 to make room for the new Kingsley Fields development.

A footpath leads from the end of Red Lion Lane in a northerly direction towards Reaseheath. About halfway along stood Kingsley Fields Farm which became part of the Reaseheath College property and was lived in by college staff in the 1950s. It later became derelict and was demolished in the early 1980s.

11. Whitehall

New houses known as 1–4 Whitehall have recently been built on the site of an Elizabethan mansion called Whitehall. This was the principal residence of the Wettenhall family who originated from Wettenhall and came to live in Nantwich around 1500. The Wettenhall family had a long and close involvement in the town affairs and this association lasted for almost 300 years.

The earliest reference to the house is in the record of a fire in the church registers in 1629. This started by the careless use of a candle in a room over the gateway in the buildings that were between the house and the roadway. The fire was confined to the roof of three bays and does not appear to have affected the mansion.

In the Nantwich Rate Books of 1792, Thomas Wettenhall is listed as living here. In 1798, the house was sold to John Jasper Garnett Esq. He resold it to John Stephens esq. of Cholmondeley, by whose will of 1811, it was left to his grand-daughter, Elizabeth Ursula Kent (née Clarke), wife of Dr William Kent, surgeon. Dr Kent lived here until his death in 1831, after which, Dr Richard Hughes, surgeon became the occupier. The 1851 Census shows Dr Hughes living here with two servants. After the death of Mrs Kent in 1855, the house was shared by the surviving family who sold it around 1865 to James Talbot, currier. An adjoining brewhouse and laundry were demolished around this time and a new house erected by Mr Talbot. These may be the premises that were destroyed by fire some years later.

In 1876 Whitehall was owned by William Cooper, tanner, and it was the headquarters of the Nantwich Liberal Club in 1896. In 1913, Edward Bayliss, antique dealer lived here, and the antiques business continued in the family with his son Augustus, right up until his death in the early 1950s.

In 1953 the local Agricultural Engineering firm of F H Burgess bought the mansion and the field behind and established business premises on what may have been the site of stables and coach houses belonging to Whitehall. The building was very unfortunately allowed to fall into decay and was eventually, most shamefully, demolished in 1965. In an article in a *Civic Society Newsletter*, T Jackson Curry gives an interesting and informative description of the building as he remembers it.

' It was a typical example of the Tudor and Elizabethan style of "magpie" construction. An oak timber main frame, jointed and connected to take the strains and stresses of load-bearing beams and the final roof trusses which, in its early days may well have carried a thatched roof. Between the elaborate pattern of timber framing, the infilled spaces were constructed of "wattle and daub" panels (a mixture of clay and cow dung plaster between rods of willow or hazel.) The building stood some way back from the roadway and was approached by a driveway and forecourt to a central doorway. To the left was an extended wing with a separate entrance. This wing was the living quarters in more modern times and could well have been the kitchens and servants' accommodation in the distant past. To the right was the gable end to a set of rooms at right angles to the main central hall.

On entering the main door one came into the large central hall with a stone flagged floor. An oak staircase led up to a galleried landing giving access to several rooms on the first floor, while other rooms on the ground floor could well have been retiring rooms in the past. The whole of this area on the ground floor and first floor were given over to the display of the Bayliss antiques and fine art collection. All these rooms were panelled oak.

Proceeding through the hall from the front door, one came to another door opposite with stained glass panels in the windows on either side. Through this latter door one entered a large conservatory, which also had a number of coloured glass panels in the roof. As the conservatory faced south, one can imagine the effect of sunlight through the coloured glass right through into the main hall. Beyond the conservatory, where the Burgess building now stands, was a lawn with a weeping ash tree in the centre, surrounded by seats under branches. This was the real front of the house. One can well imagine the garden being laid out as a pleasure area and one can picture in the mind the scenes of the past, when the house was occupied by the "gentry" and their consorts in all the finery of the centuries when it was a private residence.'

Whitehall in the 1930s. The painted exterior is somewhat different to the original as shown on the book cover.

12. 35,37 Welsh Row

St Anne's Lane marks the western end of the ancient salt houses on the south side of Welsh Row. Therefore the above premises will have been built over remnants of the salt house workings.

The clothier's shop of Joshua Howard in 1887 was succeeded later by J R Heath right up until the 1980s. There are many artefacts from this business held in Nantwich Museum and also business accounts at the Cheshire Record Office. The building was partly demolished and an Indian Restaurant now stands on the site.

13. Middle-stych

Middle-stych or sometimes Misslesiche refers to a very ancient cistern (water course or ditch) that ran from what is now St Anne's Lane to the river. It later became a lane. It marks the southern end of the salt or wich houses that stretched from the river at Wych-house Bank up to where the Black Lion public house is now. The cistern may well have been used to convey the brine to the wich houses rather like the common cistern across the street in the Wood Streets. The recent discovery of a long wooden salt 'ship' in the Wood Street area suggests that this could have been used to convey brine in this way. In Laurence Wright's will of 1603, he bequeaths a wich house of six leads lying in Mistlesiche to Robert, one of his younger sons.

A rate book of 1691 records 23 properties in this area, including one brew house, one stable and a dye house. All must have been extremely poor as their charge was only two pence or three pence farthing, the lowest charges in the town. This area was prone to flooding, and a reference in 1655 says: 'Weever did tutche the bottom of Nantwich Bridge, drowned all Mislesich and the lower end of Welsh Roe.'

In the 1792 Nantwich Rate Book, 37 properties are recorded in this and the Wych-house Bank area. The taxes paid again are very low. All properties have since been demolished.

14. Nantwich Gas Works

Mention must be made of the town's gas works built off St Anne's Lane in this area. It appears to have been built partly over old salt works and established in 1832 by several local businessmen. In 1834 it became the property of 10 shareholders. It became Nantwich Gas Company in 1869 and continued in private hands until the early 1900s when it was taken over by the Nantwich Urban District Council. The Gas Works were demolished some 20 years ago and the area is used presently as a makeshift car park. The chemicals still present in the ground from the gas production process have made it difficult to attract buyers for development. It may be some time before the land is declared safe enough to build upon.

15. 34–40 Welsh Row

A row of four buildings fronting onto the street here was demolished around the mid 1960s. In 1861 George Mullock had a grocer's shop at No.34. A photograph taken in the late 1800s of the 'Cheshire Cat' across Second Wood Street shows that it was still a grocer's shop then. Next door was Henry Kitchen's butcher's shop in 1860, where William Malkin, ropemaker lived in 1906 and Walter Hyde, fellmonger in 1913.

At No.38 Mrs Eliza Bowyer, staymaker, dressmaker and milliner lived here in 1860, Henry Tomkinson, hairdresser in 1887, Mrs Anne Williams was the shopkeeper in 1906, and in 1913 Mr F Powell, photographer and picture framer. It was still in the family by 1939.

At No.40, Emily Pike, seamstress in 1860, Thomas Dunning, stationer in 1887, Mrs Agnes Stockton, stationer and newsagent in 1906, then Mrs Powell, costumier lived here in 1913. Some time later it came into the occupation of the Ecob family, motor engineers who remained there until at least 1964. Their garage was across the road in St. Anne's Lane.

The gable-end advertising Ecob's Garage marks the end of a row of cottages since demolished. Modern houses have been built in their place.

Heath's clothing shop in the 1980s, now converted into an Indian Restaurant.

16. First and Second Wood Street

Some of the oldest salt houses in the town were established in the Wood Street area producing salt from the brine pit across the river Weaver. The earliest reference to Wood Street is in 1353. In a plan of the land occupied by wich (or salt) houses in 1624, George Twigg shows that there were something like 60 properties all producing salt in this small area. This plan was derived from details of a survey of walling, (salt making) land in the Cholmondeley Family Papers. He shows a row of plots each having an individual wich house for salt making along the river bank. Behind this row was the street that we know as First Wood Street and was then called Great Wood Street, then a further row of wich houses behind which was the common cistern conveying the brine from the salt pit across the river to the salt houses. There were just a few wich houses on the western side of the common cistern and then Little Wood Street which is what we now call Second Wood Street. A copy of this map can be seen in Nantwich Museum.

The Wood Streets are surprisingly not specifically listed in the Town Rates Book of 1691. In 1792, 35 properties are listed in First Wood Street including a smithy, a house, garden, barn and two stables belonging to Macclesfield School and a dye house. There were 43 properties in Second Wood Street including a shop, a skinner's shop, a slaughter-house and a malt kiln. With such a high number of houses in a small area it is not surprising that there was overcrowding leading later to slum conditions. In 1822 and 1833, the Weaver Brewery of Paton, Gladstone and Wordley was operating on the site previously occupied by the wich house owned by Macclesfield School.

Old black and white cottages in Wood Street.

It is believed that the cholera epidemic began in the Wood Street area in June 1849. It was particularly severe in the localities near the river and among the lower classes, although it appears that the local Irish population who lived here, managed to escape the worst of the plague. Some of the Irish men had come over to operate the last remains of the salt works probably in the Wood Street areas. These eventually closed in 1856.

In William Lee's Report to the General Board of Health on the Township of Nantwich concerning the state of sanitation at the time of the epidemic, conditions in drainage and house construction in Second Wood Street are described 'as bad as possible.... There had been cholera in most of the houses, and that two years since there was much typhus fever.'

Aware of the need to provide education for poor children in the Wood Street area, Foster Blackburne, vicar of St. Mary's, persuaded the Management Committee of Church Schools to open a school and mission in Second Wood Street in 1874. The building still stands but is now used as a garage. Many of the cottages were still standing in 1939 and 1953 but soon after were demolished and the inhabitants transferred into the relatively new council houses in the Manor Road and Wallfields area.

Old black and white cottages in Wood Street.

17. 19 Welsh Row

The present retail premises of Mia Stanza at the above address were at one time the site of Matthew Boyer's bakehouse and an advert in *Johnson's Almanac* in the early 1900s claims that it had been in use as a bakehouse for upwards of 200 years. John Boyer was the occupier in 1792, followed by Richard Boyer in 1833 and Matthew in 1850 until at least 1896. In 1913 Joseph has taken over until at least 1939 after which time it appears that the family left. It later became a garage before its present recent owners.

18. 2,4 Welsh Row

A gap in the buildings between the town bridge and Clough's shop is where No.2 Welsh Row was situated. In 1861, John Heap, shoe manufacturer lived here with three in the family. In 1896, Charles Tilsley, general dealer was here and in 1913, R Astles, tobacconist and stationer. In 1939, it was Bertie Shaw's fishing tackle shop. The building was demolished some time after this.

At No.4 was William Growcott, grocer, in 1861 and in 1896 Miss Lucy Dean, milliner. In 1913 M Lockett, confectioner, and in 1939 to 1964 it was Lilly May Fleet's sweet shop, this was then absorbed into what is now Clough's shop.

Welsh Row, Matthew Boyer and his family stand outside his bakehouse.

19. St Anne's Chapel and clock

There is a mention of St Anne's Chapel in Hall, in which he says that it was actually situated on the town bridge in 1438. This would be an oratory for a priest who offered prayers for the safety of people crossing the bridge for a payment. In 1774, Partridge mentions a clock called St Anne's, which was fixed on a dwelling in the middle of the street, which '...due to a recent alteration in the buildings there has been taken away.' The location of this building is unknown.

Nantwich Town Bridge, behind which can be seen Nos.2 and 4 Welsh Row. On the gable-end is an advert for Watson's Garage which was situated in front of Townsend House.

2 Swine Market, Snow Hill, Cart Lake, Wall Lane, Oat Market

1. 1–5 Swine Market

The area from the eastern bank of the River Weaver to the western edge of Swine Market and Wall Lane including Snow Hill is known to have been used for the manufacture of salt from very early times. The plan of wich houses in 1624, drawn by George Twigg in 1996, shows the existence of a Heating House on this site. The purpose of a Heating House is somewhat obscure but Heating House Meadow did exist to the north of the property at the edge of the wich houses.

More recently, Charles Grocott, cheese factor and rennet and annatto supplier, lived at Nos.1–3 Swine Market between 1869 and 1883 and Thomas Fowles, auctioneer, ironmonger and house furnisher lived at Nos. 1–5 Swine market in 1887 and 1896.

The showrooms contained every assortment of furniture in oak, ash, walnut, mahogany and enamel, while bedsteads and bedding, carpets, hearth and skin rugs, bamboo furniture and poles, dining, drawing and bedroom suites were also available. He also offered the largest stocks of lamps in the district, along with kitchen and culinary requisites, fenders, fire-irons, tin ware and general ironmongery.

In 1913 at No.1 Swine Market was James Hyde, butcher and there was also a butcher here in 1939. At No.5 Swine Market in 1913 lived Teddy Pace, tinsmith and town crier. Dorothy Vaughan, writing in her book *Nantwich – It Was Like This*, in 1987, quotes him as saying at difficult times: 'A pinch of snuff and God's good fresh air will pull us through.'

Sid Simpson, writing a little later in 1990 in his book *Within Living Memory* called him public lecturer and orator No.1. He would stand on the square and regale passers by with any subject under the sun, not worrying if people were listening!

2. The White Lion, No.7 Swine Market

The earliest record of this building shows it to have been an alehouse in 1774. Its licence ran continuously from that year until 1929 when it closed due to lack of trade. In 1792 it was owned by Mr Rudyard and the publican was William Parkes. In 1876 the publican was Joseph Edwards and it was described as a brewhouse, stable and public house. In 1888 an advertisement offers dog carts, phaetons and wagonettes for hire at a moment's notice. After 1929 it became a private house and was eventually demolished with the other houses in Swine Market and Snowhill in the early 1960s.

Diagram based on the Ordnance Survey 25in map of 1910

Swine Market, Snowhill, Wall Lane, Oatmarket

1 1-5 Swine Market
2 The White Lion
3 The Roebuck
4 16-30 Swine Market
5 Snow Hill
6 Cart Lake
7 The Round House

8 2-30 Wall Lane
9 36-40 Wall Lane
10 Wallfields Farm
11 1-13 Wall Lane
12 Island site – Swine Market, Oat Market
13 Oat Market East

14 12-14 Oat Market

The White Lion, Swinemarket. Woolworths now stands on this site.

3. The Roebuck

According to Dr A J MacGregor, in his book *The Inns and Innkeepers of Nantwich* in 1992, the first licence for this alehouse was awarded in 1765 when the licensee was Thomas Coventry. It later became the property of the Grocott family. MacGregor continues:

'In 1909 it was referred for closure under the Compensation Act of 1904. The report stated that its licence was unnecessary, and that the house had become the resort of poachers. Moreover, Mrs Grocott had permitted drunkenness on the premises the previous year... The report of 1909 mentioned that the inn had four bedrooms, and a stable for eight horses. Presumably the stable was the building adjoining the house on its south side. The building survived until 1933; in which year a Compulsory Purchase Order was placed upon it in furtherance of street improvement.'

4. 16–30 Swine Market

The 1792 Town Rate Books indicate the presence of a bakehouse at No. 16, and the 1851 Town Map shows the existence of a slaughterhouse immediately behind the premises.

In Hall, a serious fire on Snow Hill is referred to:

'A few minutes before two o'clock one hot July afternoon, Friday 31st 1868, Jimmy O'Neill was working in his smithy when a stray spark set fire to the thatched roof of a neighbouring stable. It was a very windy afternoon and the burning thatch was blown across the street and, in only half an hour, the fire spread from Snow Hill along the Swine Market to reach Mr Carrington's shop at the corner of High Street. It had been a very long dry summer, causing a water shortage and none could be obtained from Baddiley Mere. Everyone was greatly alarmed at the speed at which the flames were spreading, but at last the firemen and watermen ran out the old engine and water from the town was used to fight the fire. The damage however was extensive, six houses, four stables and the smithy all being destroyed, as well as five other houses losing their roofs. As a result of this tragic occurrence the Nantwich Volunteer Fire Brigade was formed.'

A look at the 1851 map of Nantwich shows the smithy, houses and stables to have been here, and it would appear that the row of houses from No.16 to No.30 were built soon after 1868. The later house at No.16 was occupied by Mrs. Elizabeth Dalton, grocery and provision dealer in 1913, but was demolished possibly at the same time as the Roebuck c1933. William Lightfoot the stonemason lived at No. 26. There was a small gap in the terrace between Nos. 26 and 28. The row of cottages was demolished with the whole of the Snow Hill area in the early 1960s.

5. Snow Hill

It is known that the area of Snow Hill was heavily involved in the manufacture of salt from the Roman era onwards. The Twigg Plan of Wich Houses in 1624 shows just how intensive the production area was. However it was declining by the mid 17th century and by 1713 it is known that the wich houses here had either been demolished or were in a very bad state of repair.

The 1792 Rate Book lists 38 different properties in this area, several of which were stables. It is difficult to identify individual houses even with the aid of the 1851 Map. A row of cottages, Nos.2–20 Snow Hill, were built behind and at right angles to 16–28 Swine Market, probably at the same time. Then Nos.22–28 Snow Hill were part of a small row at right angles to these near Wall Lane. Nos.9–35 formed the northern edge of Snow Hill. Nos.21–29 were demolished some time before the 1930s.

Peter Clough, who lived at No.11 Snow Hill gives his memories of childhood here from 1939 to 1954:

'My earliest memory of Snowhill is of being made to stand with my mother in Tommy Owen's garden on the top of Snowhill bank to watch the big bonfire the older lads had lit to celebrate Guy Fawkes night. This was around the mid-1940s, I would be about four years old at the time.

Young lads and girls like myself, namely, Alan Slater, Alan and Norman Nevitt, John and Dave Cork, Les and Ken Stubbs, Pat, Glenys and Tommy Moore, Michael Shuker, Margaret Hope, John and Tom Dutton, Bill Blackburn, Barbara Wright and Albert Pye, who lived on Snowhill or Wall Lane found plenty of places to play in.

The old swimming baths at the bottom of the bank, empty of water but the white tiles of the pool area still in place. The engine-house. Just a pile of rubble covered with shrubs and brambles. We used to make camps in amongst it all. Tin sheets for the sides, wall-to-wall carpeting (old sacks and lino), cover the top with planks and earth, candles for lighting and what had you got? Heaven!

The dug-out at the top of Cartlake. It was an air-raid shelter built in a U-shape. It was pitch-black inside. We used to go through it with the older lads and it frightened us to death! The "Salt Mine" on the top of the bank was our fort. It was split into four sections with a central well down which we hid our bonfire stuff.

A Mr Henson who lived in Cartlake had two greyhounds and one hot summer's day, he was exercising them on the field next to our house. My mother was at home on her lunch break from work when one of the dogs came straight through the open front door, snatched what was left of the Sunday roast and went out of the back. Mr. Henson was very apologetic and compensated my mother with half a dozen fresh eggs.

Going back to bonfire night, there was always great rivalry with us and the Wood Street lads on trying to steal each other's bonfire collections. One time Wood Street had their bonfire piled up ready for the big day and we decided to try the old Red Indian trick and shoot flaming arrows across the river at it. I don't think any even got across!

On the night of the Coronation we had a bonfire of our own on Snowhill bank. The blaze was seen by someone who thought that the old Town Hall was going up and rang the Fire Brigade. Our celebrations were consequently washed right down the hill!

The Old Lock-Up (Police Station) was still there in those days. Then it was a Lodging House, but later two families, the Lees and the Moores moved in and it became a private dwelling.

Mellor's scrapyard was always a busy place and in the evenings when Harry Mellor had locked up and gone home, we were over the fence and playing in the yard. Just past Mellor's and across the Gannel Entry (the narrow passage between the old Town Hall and Howard's shop) I can remember two old stables. The horses were long gone and the place was in a derelict state but horse collars and brasses were still hanging on the wall.

Joe Moore, who lived at No. 13, would go out early in the mornings across Kingsley Fields to collect mushrooms and watercress that he would sell at the Red Lion (at the corner of Swine and Oat Markets) for the price of a pint.

Frank Slater at No.19 was a big pigeon fancier and had a big pigeon-cote at the bottom of his garden. He didn't like us making too much noise when his birds were landing after a race in case we frightened them off.

Nos. 22–28 had a communal cellar. We had found a way into it and I think it must also have been used as a stable at some time in the past as there were bits of horse trappings hanging about. We had to be very quiet while we were down there because the families above could hear us.

By 1964 it had all gone and families who had lived side by side for years were dispersed all over the town. Now we are left with a large car park but at least they can't take away our memories!'

RESIDENTS IN SNOWHILL IN 1939:

No.2	John Dawson
No.4	Mary Hockenhull
No.6	Ann Davies
No.8	Charles Burrows
No.10	Evelyn Clarke
No.12	Mary Lloyd
No.14	Robert Campbell
No.16	Ernest Matthews
No.18	Wilfred Harvey
No.20	George Nevitt
No.22	George Davies
No.24	Georgina Batho
No.26	John Hope
No.28	Thomas Hassall
No.35	James Sherratt
No.33	Mary Bott
No.31	Arthur Hammersley
No.21	Louisa Basford
No.19	Frank Slater
No.17	Frederick Hope
No.15	John Hough
No.13	Joseph Moore
No.11	William Clough
No. 9	Fred. Flowers
Old Lock-Ups	John Bradshaw Lodging House

RESIDENTS IN 1964

No.2	Tommy Owen
No.4	Nora Seller
No.6	E Cartwright
No.8	Ray Davenport
No.10	Evelyn Clarke
No.14	D Jones
No.20	Horace Flory

6. Cart Lake

Cart Lake was originally a large pool that received the water from the Lothburn (or Lamporn) drain or channel. This channel commenced in the Churchyardside flowing between Pepper Street and what is now Market Street, crossing Beam Street, along Dog Lane and then turning at right angles to flow behind property in Beam Street and emptying into Cart Lake. Part of this channel is shown on the Pepper Street Map.

In 1840, Cart Lake was about 30 feet in diameter and had become a filthy cesspool. Hall refers to a ducking stool here at one time. More recently a short street running diagonally from the end of Beam Street at the back of the Roebuck to the northern part of Snow Hill was known as Cart Lake. In 1861, Joseph Butters, cordwainer, John Lightfoot, stonemason, and John Hinson, shoemaker all lived here. Nos. 2 and 4 Cart Lake were occupied in 1939 and 1953.

7. The Round House

This most interesting building is thought to have been erected around 1800 replacing the previous Gaol House in Pillory Street. The Round House was not round but square. However this was a term generally used at that time for a small country lock-up usually with no windows and light being admitted via a domed roof, hence the name.

In Hall's Notebooks, he writes:

'It was altered when Laxton came, (Charles Laxton was Nantwich's first High Constable) there were no railings around and it was approached by steps. There was also a pair of stocks. It was kept at the beginning of the century by Harry Robinson. In war times, deserters were put there on their way to Chester. It was the Nantwich House of Correction, there was no Knutsford jail then.'

In Hall there is a further reference to the Round House:

'On 17th Dec.1828 a number of Nantwich shoemakers and others of the town and neighbourhood were implicated in a great poaching affray on the Darnhall estate, causing much excitement in the town... the ringleaders were apprehended in the Round House on Snow Hill. They were tried at Chester; six or seven were sentenced to fourteen year's transportation and the rest to short terms of imprisonment. Through a technical flaw in the indictment, the same not specifying whether the offence was committed after twelve at noon, or twelve at night... they were liberated after some months' imprisonment on board the *Justicia* convict hulk at Woolwich.'

In 1832, two shoemakers who were officials in the newly formed Nantwich Shoemakers Society were arrested and lodged in the Round House prior to trial at Chester for belonging to a trade union. The full tale is a fascinating insight into the difficult times suffered by those involved in the early days of trade unionism. The Post Office at that time was at the Lamb Hotel and in order not to arouse suspicion by the Magistrate's Clerk who frequented the hostelry, Thomas Dunning walked every Sunday to Chester to post letters to Dublin. As he arrived by breakfast time, he must have left Nantwich about 3 or 4 o'clock. It was to Dublin that Thomas Dunning had sent William Capper (the only witness for the trial) to keep him out of the way. The trial was eventually dismissed due to lack of evidence (the only witness could not be traced.)

In *The Life of Charles Laxton – High Constable of Police, Nantwich* written in 2003, Pauline Horner refers to the move of the Laxton family to Snow Hill:

'In 1848 the salt baths on Snow Hill, which had been there only a short time, were removed. In addition the nearby old prison, known as the Round House, which in spite of its name was a rectangular building, was also taken down and a new police office and prison erected on its site. Adjoining this, a residence for Charles and his family was built.

The last criminal detained in the Round House was Mary Gallop, for poisoning her father at Crewe. She was hanged at Chester in 1844. In the new prison on the site, the first and only murderer confined, prior to her trial at Chester, was Sarah Featherstone, for the murder of her child. She was condemned to be executed but respite was granted and she was imprisoned for life.'

In 1851 there were four prisoners in the cells when the Census was carried out. When a new constabulary was built in 1860 on the garden of Townsend House, the Round House ceased to function as a police office. By 1861 Charles Laxton had moved to other premises at 48 Welsh Row. The old Lock Ups, as they came to be known eventually became a Lodging House in 1939 and were still standing in 1953. They were demolished at the same time as the rest of Snow Hill in the early 1960s.

8. 2–30 Wall Lane

The 1691 Nantwich Rate Books lists 27 properties in Wall Lane. The only possible identifier is the reference to Richard Colbach occupying a house and skin house. This could possibly be a reference to the tannery, which we know was situated on the site of what is now Delmar Press. In 1789 the tannery owner was Robert Taylor and prior to that possibly a Mr Robinson. The occupier in 1792 was Robert Burgan. The properties in this tanyard area are described as 'House , Garden, Stable, Tanyard, and Croft as under Mr Walthall's Land, Mr Wickstead's Part, Hays's Croft and that part of Yard where Bark Stacks stand and ... Limehouse at end.' The 1851 map clearly shows the tannery with 21 lime pits for soaking the hides, set back from the road. The tannery appears to have closed around 1855. There is a saw pit shown at the back of what was the lime house, on the 1874 map.

In Hall's Notebooks in 1876, Mr Johnson owns and occupies the tan house. Thomas Downes occupies the yard, offices, warehouse and land, and the owners were John and W W Downes.

There was a row of cottages stretching from behind the timber yard on the corner of Beam Street and Wall Lane to the tannery on the 1851 map. According to Johnson, this was described as:

Old black and white cottages in Wall Lane, painted in 1907.

'A jumble of old property mainly consisting of the worst type of Elizabethan hovels, originally built without upper rooms; to these cock-lofts had been later added with small windows through thatched roofs; access was up a step-ladder stair.'

In 1898 he attended a fire there and assisted in their demolition, but leaving the two brick-built cottages at the end of the row, these being eventually demolished c1970. Five cottages down from the Beam Street end was an entry and this led to three cottages in a yard behind the row previously mentioned.

9. 36–40 Wall Lane

Three black and white cottages were situated here of similar construction to those referred to in the above paragraph. They were destroyed by fire around 1932 and three brick built houses were erected in their place the following year. A stone tablet on the present middle cottage reads 'Weaver View 1933.'

10. Wallfields Farm

In 1792, the farm was owned by Peter Walthall and occupied by Samuel Fitton. In 1834, 1841 and 1846 the occupier was Thomas Rowley and the owner was James Walthall Hammond of Wistaston Hall. In 1861 the occupier was William Green, Mrs Jane Green in 1874 and Sampson Cartwright in 1881. Shortly after, the tenant was P H Chesters, the grocer. His staff and apprentices lived there. At the rear of the farm were shippens, and stables for the horses that took his provisions around the country area. There was an approach from Dog Lane. The farm later came into the possession of the Broomhall family of butchers and the buildings were demolished in the 1920s.

Wallfields Farm. Houses in Malbank now stand where this stood. It was once owned by P.H.Chesters and later by Broomhall's the butchers.

11. 1–13 Wall Lane

There was a row of cottages here leading from the Beam Street end towards Wallfields on the west side of Wall Lane. These had been demolished by 1910.

12. Swine Market/Oat Market Island site

Houses and shops on the island site have proved somewhat difficult to identify because of shared addresses with High Street and Oat Market. The only reference to No. 2 Swine Market is in 1896 when it was occupied by E C Gilbert, watchmaker.

At No. 4 Swine Market were licensed premises that had started as an alehouse in 1775 known as The King's Head. Its licence ran continuously until 1906 when it became one of the first casualties in the town of the 1904 Compensation Act. There was a name change to The Goat's Head in 1828 and then shortly after, in 1834, it became finally The Nantwich Arms. According to MacGregor:

'At the Brewster Sessions of 1894 an application for the transfer of the licence... was refused. The Justices complained that the inn had become a drinking place only, and pointed out that within a 63-yard radius from the Nantwich Arms there were eight other licensed houses. In spite of their reservations, the house survived for twelve more years... In 1906... it had been referred for closure. It was stated that " the licence is unnecessary." Only drink was supplied on the premises, no food. Sales of beer averaged only three barrels a week; and there had been ten tenants in the last ten years.'

Vaughan refers to some of the buildings in both Swine and Oat Market.

'The floors inside them slanted quite a lot, e.g. Davies' fish and chip shop had two steps up from Swine Market and three steps down from Oat Market. Jesse Sutton (picture framer) and Jack Basford (barber) had their shop fronts facing Oat Market. The wedge of buildings culminated in the Red Lion Inn at the Beam Street end. None of these buildings had even a backyard, so all washing had to be dried indoors (no spin dryers then!).

In the early part of the 20th century the Red Lion was licensed under ancient laws, which meant that the landlord could not refuse shelter or food to man or beast. It was open from 6am to midnight for grooms passing through. They were served with rum and coffee at 6am. Frank Mason, the landlord, had to call on Job Edge of the Crown Hotel to furnish stabling for the horses. The three cellars at the Red Lion were noted as the best in the town, because the landlord was fanatical about cleanliness and order. This inn had four front doors, but no back ones. Every Thursday night at 8pm the nightsoil cart was due on its rounds, and one customer would keep a look-out for it, so that the doors could be closed while it passed.'

The Red Lion opened sometime after 1775 and its licence ran continuously until closure in 1950. In the application for transfer of the licence in 1948, to the present Red Lion on the Barony, the public house was described as the 'shaking inn,' because: 'At the present time buses had to go up a very narrow street and the property was being shaken about.'

Johnson remembers a small boot shop next to the Nantwich Arms, kept by John Cope who was also a country postman and then adjoining, before the Red Lion was Mrs Merga an Italian straw bonnet maker. The whole of the island site was demolished around 1959.

The Red Lion in Swinemarket/Oatmarket. It had four front doors and no back door. In the distance can be seen cottages in Swinemarket.

Jack Basford outside his hairdressers and tobacconist shop in Oatmarket.

13. Oat Market Eastern side

There were at one time two cottages in front of the Talbot (now the Frog and Ferret). In the right-hand cottage may have lived a scissor grinder and in the other lived two real Nantwich characters, Billy and Jacky Bowyer, twin brothers. Billy was a barber and had a shop on the western end of the island site block of shops in the square, later demolished. Jacky was a tailor.
  Willett describes them thus:

> 'They were both dressed alike in the ancient style of the 18th century; knee breeches, grey wool stockings, low shoes with broad toes, low heels and fastened with silver buckles. Low flat-brimmed black felt hats, silver watches, with the chain hanging down, and as they proceeded in slow dignified manner to church every Sunday, each with a Bible and Prayer Book under his arm, let me tell you it was a sight fit for the gods!'

Johnson also remembers them:

> '... two elf-like characters, Jacky and Billy Boyer, a barber and a tailor; the front door was approached up three steep stone steps jutting into Oat Market.
>   These two odd men were well-known characters and butts for practical jokers. One day when painters' ladders were reared against our shop adjoining, there was a cry of 'fire' and smoke was seen issuing from Billy Boyer's door, the two brothers carrying buckets of water into the house; a cry was soon raised by the crowd, 'Billy, there's a bag on thi chimbly top'; a small boy had been provided with a bag of paper shavings and incited to put it there; the culprit was discovered and I remember the sequel.'

14. 12/14 Oat Market

At No.12 Oat Market lived Jack Hammersley shoemaker. He had a grocer's shop here in 1896. Next door at No.14 lived Jack O'Hara, scissor grinder. His wife Mary was a specialist at light cakes and made them for all the confectioners in the town. Adjoining the premises in 1896 was White Brothers, tailors and clothiers. By 1913 Purcell and Blackburn, tailors had occupied the premises.

15. The Ship Inn

It is well known that the Ship Inn was destroyed in the fire of 1583 and rebuilt soon after. The owner was Richard Walthall and the tenant was Ralph Seckerston. As there were only six properties affected, it is assumed that these could all have been on the eastern side of Love Lane (as it was then called). This could then place the Inn somewhere near what is now the Frog and Ferret. The owner's contribution to the rebuilding was £100, which was a substantial sum in those days, suggesting a large property.
  Hall suggests that William Cappur may have kept the Ship in 1666, due to the existence of a halfpenny token dated 1666 and with a ship engraved on the reverse side. The 1664 Hearth Tax shows that William Cappur had six hearths, again pointing to a large house.
  There is one further reference, and this is in the Wilbraham Papers from which Hall quotes an extract 'The next day (5 Dec. 1723) there happened a fire in a house late Madews, next door to the Ship alehouse; which threatened much damage to the town.'
  There is a reference to an unnamed alehouse in Oat Market in MacGregor whose licence ran from 1796 to 1814, but there is no definite evidence that links it to the Ship other than the curious fact that Charles Capper was the licensee in 1806.

3 BEAM STREET

1. 2–8 Beam Street

Modern shops have replaced older buildings at this end of Beam Street. It is undoubtedly one of the oldest parts of the town and the fire of 1583 is known to have destroyed property here.

In 1792, No. 2 Beam Street is described as House, Joiner's Shop, Yard at back of Joiner's Shop and Grocer's Shop. It was owned by Messers Hockenhull and Davies and occupied by William Davies. In 1833 it was owned by John Bolland and in the occupation of William Buckley. In 1876 it was occupied by William Fowles, auctioneer and broker. In 1896 it was in the possession of White Brothers, clothiers and in 1913, Purcell and Blackburn, tailors and cutters. In 1939 it was Steven Clarke, Fish and Chip shop. Some time after this, the building was demolished.

The Royal Oak with its landlady, Eva Wainwright Stubbs outside. A room here was used as a recruiting office during the Napoleonic Wars.

Diagram based on the Ordnance Survey 25in map of 1910

Beam Street

1 2-8 Beam Street
2 1-5 Beam Street
3 9-11 Beam Street
4 22-62 Beam Street
5 Gilbert s Shoe Factory
6 Dog Lane
7 37-39 Beam Street
8 64-66 Beam Street
9 The Technical Institute
10 The Fire Station
11 57/59-121 Beam Street
12 68a-130 Beam Street
13 Mainwaring s Mansion

At No. 4 Beam Street was The Royal Oak public house until 1983 when it was demolished. Its licence ran continuously from 1765, beginning as an alehouse. According to Hall, it was formerly called The Star Inn, and one room, known for ages as the soldier's parlour, was used as a recruiting office during the Napoleonic Wars, where many a country yokel was enticed to accept the 'King's Shilling.' According to Simpson, meetings of the Giant Onion Society were held here at the Royal Oak.

In 1792, No. 6 Beam Street is described as a Malt Kiln, but in 1833 it had become a house in the occupation of Mrs Lockett and owned by James Westmore. In 1896, Joseph Willett, bootmaker lived here, and in 1913, Henry Bourne, Baths Manager.

At No. 8 Beam Street was the Talbot public house. This began as an alehouse in 1774 and its licence ran continuously until 1883 when it closed. In 1856 and 1857 it was referred to as the Dog, a common nickname for public houses in the County called the Talbot. It was also called the Golden Talbot and the Old Talbot to distinguish it from the newer Talbot in Oat Market. It changed its name to the Peacock in 1857. According to Johnson, there was a skittle alley in the entry at the side of the property.

2. 1–5 Beam Street

A black and white cottage adjacent to the Roebuck and facing the street has variously been described as being No.1 Beam Street. It was here that George Henson had his mews, with stabling for horses behind. His wife had a sweet shop. According to Simpson, horses from Henson's were sometimes used for the fire brigade. Henson's also had brakes and cabs for excursions and ran a weekend service to Crewe.

Across Cartlake on an island site was Thorley's the greengrocer. In 1939 this had become Ormes and Yates, sweets and tobacconist's shop. Across Wall Lane on the corner was a timber yard in 1851. Later on, stabling for the Royal Oak was provided here. Behind here in 1954 was Preston's garage. Although not absolutely clear, it may be that James Bowyer had a shop here in 1896, and possibly, J Moorhouse, fried fish and chip dealer in 1913.

At No.3 Beam Street in 1896 lived James Purcell, tripe dresser and in 1913, William Adams, cycle maker, agent and repairer.

At No.5 Beam Street was Joseph Willett, boot and clog manufacturer in 1896, he was known as 'Clogger Willett.' In 1913, the occupier was George Robinson, boot and clog manufacturer, also known as 'Clogger Robinson.' This later became Robinson's shoe shop continuing in existence until c1970. The Robinsons had a shoe manufacturing factory in Market Street.

Right: John Worrell's Posting Mews, 1 Beam Street. This thatched black and white cottage stood where The Pizza Place and Home Farm Trust shops are now.

3. 9,11 Beam Street

In 1792, No.9 Beam Street was a private house owned and lived in by Mrs Hayles. At some time before 1833, it had become the Red Cow, its licence being transferred from the original Red Cow at 7a Beam Street. Its licensee in 1833 was James Smith. It became known as The Old Red Cow when James Smith took the licence with him to the new premises at 55 Beam Street shortly after 1833. It was called The Modern Druid's Arms around 1850 and The Lingard Arms c1881. According to MacGregor:

'In 1909 this fully-licensed house was referred for closure under the Compensation Act of 1904. It was stated that the building was an old house and not suitable for licensed premises; and that it was difficult for the police to supervise (presumably because of the large garden to the rear). Moreover there were already four fully-licensed houses and two beerhouses in Beam Street.'

In 1913 it had become Blackburn's Cycle Stores and a year later it was the premises of Enoch Moulton, greengrocer, fruiterer and florist. This continued in existence until the building was eventually demolished c1959 along with the Nag's Head Public House next door.

At No. 11 Beam Street was The Nag's Head Public House, with a continuous licence running from 1767 until its closure c1955. It had a terracotta horses head figure over the doorway. In 1792, it is described as The Nag's Head Public House with a Yard, Stables, Garden and Smithy. Later, in 1891, the brewing firm of Greenall Whitley had bought the property. It was demolished along with its neighbouring property c1959.

Enoch Moulton's greengrocers shop decorated for a coronation or jubilee, on the corner of Manor Road. Manor House can be seen on the opposite corner.

Enoch Moulton standing outside his shop. This building was licensed as an alehouse called the Red Cow. It later changed its name to The Druid's Arms and The Lingard Arms before closing as a public house in 1909.

The Nag's Head. Note the terracotta horse's head above the front door.

4. 22–62 Beam Street

A row of cottages, interspersed with a few shops, was to be found between the end of Pepper Street and Market Street. These have all been demolished and replaced with modern shops. At the corner of Pepper Street, at No. 22 Beam Street, in 1876 and 1896 was Henry Sumner, hairdresser. No. 26 Beam Street was a bakehouse in 1792, and a baby linen shop in 1876. At No. 30 Beam Street in 1913 was A E Glover, hairdresser. In 1939 this had become Glover's sweetshop, continuing in existence until the late 1950s. In 1961, the sweetshop was being run by M & H Bradshaw, and in 1969 and 1974 by A E White.

Vaughan refers to shops in this row:

'Crossing the end of Market Street, perhaps a smell wafted on the breeze would tell us that we were approaching the shop of Mrs Parkes. She was a fussy little woman, who sold sweets and groceries, but was also famed for her cooked meats, etc. especially savoury ducks called 'ducks i' veels' (ducks in veils). A few doors on, Mrs Walker made and sold cakes and toffee and a little distance beyond was William Wardby's shop (groceries and sweets) with Barber Glover's shop adjoining.'

The row was demolished some time around 1980.

Nantwich Carnival procession in 1966 showing Yvonne Ormes as Miss Nantwich. Behind her are two typical Nantwich cottages, at 24 and 26 Beam St.

Nantwich Carnival procession in 1966 with Glover's sweetshop behind.

5. Gilbert's Shoe Factory

In the yard at the rear of the entry between what is now Broomhall's butchers shop and Hilton's Tea Rooms was E C Gilbert's shoe factory. This is shown on the 1875 Ordnance Survey Map as a long narrow building, stretching back from the rear of what is now Hilton's Tea Rooms. This building was most likely Claypole's shoe factory that was destroyed by fire on 4 July 1920.

6. Dog Lane

The Playhouse at the back of the Shakespeare was built early in the 19th century according to Hall. Apparently it was a fairly nondescript building. With the death of Charles Mare, patron, and the decline in popularity with the theatregoing public, the theatre closed and was partly demolished in 1840. The gallery was converted into The Oddfellows Lodge Room and a row of cottages built on the site of the pit, stage and green-room. This row of cottages survived until the early 1960s. There was also one other cottage on the opposite side of Dog Lane.

7. 37,39 Beam Street

At No. 37 lived Mrs Sarah Davis in 1896, in 1913 it was Robert Moulton, labourer, in 1953, J W Dean, and R Simpson in 1961. Next door at No. 39 was a blacksmith's shop in 1876. In 1896, the smith was James Welch. In 1913, he is described as engineer, machinist and general smith. In 1939 was R Perrin, motor engineer, in 1953, Perrin's Cycle Depot, in 1961 it was occupied by The Crewe School of Motoring and in 1971, the Classic School of Motoring. Both properties were demolished some time soon after this.

8. 64,66 Beam Street

At 64 Beam Street, on the corner of Market Street where the bus station is now, was the Market Tavern. According to MacGregor:

> 'It was a beerhouse formerly owned by Lord Tollemache... Its stables, which could accommodate up to 15 horses, stood in Market Street and its back door opened onto the same thoroughfare. It was referred for closure in 1923. The report into the condition of the property stated that the premises were structurally deficient and unsuitable for a licensed house. Because of its being open to the rear, it was difficult for police supervision. When the house was full of customers, the atmosphere was unpleasant because of the low ceilings.' Its licence ran from 1871 until 1923 when it closed. Vaughan refers to Edward Tomkinson, the licensee from 1890 to 1914, as 'Cetch'em Tomkinson.' Apparently when he was short of customers, he would rattle the dominoes and say 'This'll cetch'em.'

Next door at No. 66, around the same time was the Cotton-Jodrell Day Nursery for working mothers. This was a tall, narrow house. Both properties were demolished in 1924 as part of a street improvement scheme.

9. The Technical Institute

The Technical Institute was built on land donated by Lord Tollemache in 1902. It was made of red Ruabon brick with stone dressings, designed by a local architect, Charles Davenport, and cost £2,500 then. It was designed to accommodate 150 students. The Urban District Council held their meetings there in 1914. In 1939 H C Barker was the Headmaster. In the last years of its life it was being used for school meals, bingo sessions, flower shows, meetings and other small social events. It was demolished c1970 and a modern library for the town now stands in its place.

Nantwich Technical Institute, built in 1902 which was used for teaching and extra-curricular activities. Nantwich Library stands on the same site.

10. The Fire Station

The 1851 Town Map shows a timber yard here. It later belonged to Richard Prince, who lived opposite, on the corner of Crowsfoot Lane. In 1896 it belonged to John Matthews, builder, contractor and timber merchant.

In 1913, Clarke and Shakeshaft, carriage builders had their premises here. By 1939 it had become the Council Depot and Fire Station for the NUDC and Ambulance Station for the Nantwich Urban and Rural District Councils. In 1974, it was the NUDC Rates Office, Council Yard and Fire Station. The buildings were later demolished, and the Fire Station moved to a new site across the road in Beam Street. A housing development called Lady Helen Walk was then built at this location.

Nantwich Fire Brigade procession showing Henry Careful's pawnbroking shop behind the right-hand fireman.

The old Nantwich Fire Station photographed in the 1980s. The two fire engines can be seen behind the doors.

11. 57/59–121 Beam Street

At the corner of the entry to Cowfields at No. 57/59 Beam Street, stood for many years, Carefull's shop. In 1913, William Henry Carefull is listed as a pawnbroker. In 1939, it had become a ladies outfitter's shop and in 1961 Mrs H Carefull is described as a draper. It was demolished some time after this. In an article in the *Nantwich Chronicle* in the early 1950s, Mrs. Carefull remembers the earlier days in the pawnbroking business:

'Mondays used to be particularly busy days and we were open from 7 o'clock in the morning to 11 o'clock at night. We had all kinds of things in pawn and our customers were certainly not confined to poor people. One woman regularly pawned a valuable diamond ring for which she was paid £10, redeeming it as her money came through.

Our strangest pledge was a farm in Ireland. Others have included a pony, a donkey and a scissor grinder's equipment. Father bought the pony for the children when its owner redeemed it.

The charges? A halfpenny for each pawn ticket, and a halfpenny interest on every two shillingsworth pledged. Pledges under ten shillings became the pawnbroker's property if not claimed within a year and seven days.'

At No. 67 Beam Street was Davies' Tripe Shop as mentioned in Vaughan:

'Every Friday evening there would be a queue of people with jugs waiting to buy the tripe at 3d. for a large piece, with broth. It was thoroughly cleaned with wire brushes on large slabs and boiled in a large boiler or 'copper'. Everything was scrupulously clean. There was also 'black' tripe available; this was prepared in a different way. Another queue would form on Sunday mornings, from 8am to 10.30am for cow heels, the charge for which was 5d.'

Further interesting insights are given of other people living in this row:

'A few yards on was Granny Poole's tiny (greengrocery) shop; she also had a stall in the market on market days. Very soon Fred Shakeshaft's cycle shop and repair works were reached, then Harry Clayton (butcher), Massey's lodging house and round the corner, behind some hoardings, Absolom (Yap) Marsh had his caravan and general dealer's yard. He was the local "Steptoe". He drove his horse and cart at a furious pace, grimacing the while and talking to the horse. He would buy and sell horses (dead or alive), all kinds of goods too, and he bought salt from Winsford, which he later sold to farmers.'

Simpson also recalls this character. 'Absolom (Yap) Marsh was often seen sitting on the carcase of a horse on the back of his long cart, taking it to his knacker's yard opposite the Almshouses.'

Johnson refers to Billy Tomlinson's Private School, which was on this corner of Beam Street:

'Billy Tomlinson's School was in an old cottage on the left hand side of Beam Street. His pupils were always in demand as clerks in solicitors' offices. One of his dictums was "no use me teaching you to write like copperplate unless you spell correctly". '

Reg Baker remembers a smithy behind the cycle shop of Shakeshafts. The garage of Ernest Pritchard occupied this site somewhat later in the 1950s.

A report on housing conditions in Nantwich in 1945 by the County Council's Public Health Department highlights the state of three houses in the row:

'The small yards of these four-roomed cottages are bounded on the north side by dilapidated wooden sheds. The brickwork of the closet structures and boundary walls is perished and defective. The internal conditions of the houses is fairly good but there are no proper pantries or coal stores. The lighting of the back kitchen of No. 99 is obstructed by a large wooden shed that is used as a scullery. The back kitchen windows in all three houses are fixed. No. 101 has non washing boiler.'

Kenneth Haley in *Recollections of Beam Street and Snowhill in the 1940s*, refers to the Town Mortuary, several yards down Volunteer Fields:

'A dismal looking red brick building with windows high up in the walls. A high hedge surrounded three sides of the building. Natural curiosity in young lads gave us the desire to peer inside. We would each give one another a "leg-up" to satisfy our curiosity. What we saw ensured that we did not continue this practice in the future.'

Around 1964, the whole row of cottages was demolished and a new housing development called King Place together with a new Police Station, were built.

12. 68a–130 Beam Street

A row of cottages, from 68a to 130 Beam Street, used to stand between the 'Tech.' and the Almshouses at the end of the street. At No. 68a, in 1896 was W Simmons, shopkeeper and grindery dealer. In 1913, was Sarah Ann Simmons, grocer. It later became Phelps, grocers and in 1939 was Phelps' sweetshop.

Between No's. 70 and 72 Beam Street a row of cottages at right angles to the street was built. This row was called Johnstone's Buildings. These cottages were demolished c1968. At

No. 74 Beam Street in 1896 and 1913, was Mrs Ann Basford, grocer. In 1939 it had become Annie Basford's sweetshop and in 1953 it was John Basford's sweetshop. At No. 78 Beam Street was James Coventry, greengrocer in 1896. In 1913 it was George Davies, shopkeeper.

The Green Man Alehouse stood somewhere near 90 Beam Street and was licensed from 1775 to 1804. Between 1784 and 1787 its name had changed to The Horse and Groom. Adjacent to this property in 1833 was an entry leading to Heath's yard in which were four cottages.

At No.94 Beam Street in 1913 was Lucy Snowball's sweetshop. By1953, some of the cottages mentioned earlier had been demolished and G & W Lea and Manweb had their yards and stores here. At No. 98 Beam Street in 1939 was James Seabridge, newsagent and in 1953 and 1961, the newsagent was Jack Lewis. Les Heath had a second-hand goods shop here from 1964 until 1967. Close to this property in 1833 was an entry leading to a yard called Broadbent's Yard in which were five cottages.

13. Mainwaring's Mansion

In Hall are references to the Mainwaring Mansion in Beam Street. He quotes directly from King's *Vale Royal* about Nantwich.

'It may not be amiss… to note one lustre of that town; that into the five entrances into the same, which way soever you come, your eye is entertained with a fair gentlemanly house at the end or entry of the first street every way: as namely… that of Beam Street, where they hold yet weekly great markets of cattle, with a fine house of the Mainwarings, and now belonging to the right worshipful and worthy ingenious knight Sir Dudley Norton, secretary to His Majesty's council in Ireland.'

Hall also provides further information about the Mansion.

'The Beam Street-End Mansion, which Sir Dudley Norton had held since his marriage, in 1591, with Margaret, daughter of Thomas Maisterson and widow of Roger Mainwaring, passed after the death of Lady Margaret Norton in 1644 to the family of Dodd of Edge, of whom it was purchased by Robert Wright, who was possessor of it in 1666. It afterwards in 1677, became the House of Correction; and was ultimately purchased by John, first Lord Crewe, who, in 1767, pulled it down and built the present almshouses on the site.'

The above named Roger Mainwaring owned a considerable number of houses in the town. Some, in Beam Street are mentioned in his Will dated 1589 and are of interest:

'I bequeath unto my loving weif Margaret Mainwaring, my chief mansion house at the townsende of Namptwiche with all the buildings and gardens appertaining,… I give etc. unto Richard Mainwaring, my eldest sonne… two messuages in Beamstrete in Namptwiche, one called the Saracen's Head, etc… one other howse in the same strete wherein my mother (Cicely) dwelleth, nexte the horsemylle of Henry Manwaringe of Carincham esquire… Unto my younger sonne John Mainwaring two howses lying togeather in the Beamstrete the one Cheynye Hall etc… and the other in the tenure of my aunte Alice Crockett wydowe.'

The references to Cheyney Hall and the Saracen's Head are of interest as they were both lost in the fire of Nantwich in1583 and replaced soon after. They were in fact next door to each other and because the fire (as far as we know) only affected the line of buildings between Oat Market and Pepper Street, these two properties could be placed within this general area.

4 Pepper Street,
Churchyardside, Market Street

1. 30–38 Pepper Street

In 1861, George Heath, shoe manufacturer lived at No.30 Pepper Street. In 1871 he had become an earthenware and grindery dealer and in 1881, a general dealer. In 1914, Thomas Barlow, estate agent, accountant, insurance agent, receiver to the Beam Heath Estate and assistant overseer is listed here. It was also, along with No.32 Pepper Street, the offices of the Urban District Council, both properties being demolished in 1928. According to Vaughan, while the foundations for the new General Post Office were being laid, a charnel pit 10 feet deep and very wide was discovered. This was filled with human and animal bones, suggesting that the church graveyard may have extended as far as this point years ago.

In 1871, at No.32 Pepper Street, lived Ann Bunn, Provision Dealer. In 1881, it was Ann Phillips, grocer, in 1892 and 1908 was William Walker, shopkeeper, and in 1913, Frank Astles, clerk.

Photograph of shops at the lower end of Pepper Street taken in the 1980s. These have been demolished and now McCormick's Café, Pockets Menswear and Baker Wynne Wilson estate agents replace them.

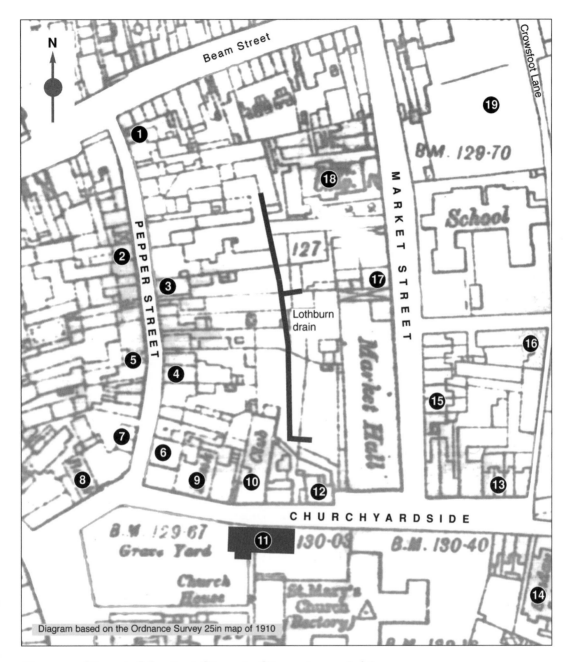

Diagram based on the Ordnance Survey 25in map of 1910

Pepper Street, Market Street, Churchyardside

1 30-38 Pepper Street

2 11-27 Pepper Street

3 16-20 Pepper Street

4 12 Pepper Street

5 9 Pepper Street

6 2-6 Pepper Street

7 1-7 Pepper Street

8 1-3 Churchyardside

9 The Midland Bank

10 The Conservative Club

11 The Old Grammar School

12 21 Churchyardside

13 23-35 Churchyardside

14 Congregational School Hall

15 2-14 Market Street

16 Shoe Factory

17 The Fire Engine House

18 The Baptist Chapel

19 Air Raid Shelter

1n 1851, at No.34 Pepper Street, lived Samuel Foden, carrier. He was there 10 years later but now described as a railway carrier. In 1871 Ann Foden is living here and is described as a retired carrier's agent and 10 years later her occupation is described as 'income from house rents'. She is still here in 1896. From 1935 until 1969, it was occupied by Edward Jones. This property was demolished along with Nos. 36 and 38 Pepper Street in the mid 1980s.

In 1881, No.36 Pepper Street was occupied by Joseph Hockenhull, Shoe Manufacturer, and in 1896 by William Walker, grocer. By 1914, it had come into the possession of John Reynolds, baker and confectioner, who baked his bread and cakes at the rear of his premises. He also had a tobacconist and sweet shop next door. He was still here in 1939, but by 1953, J J Lloyd had taken over the confectioner's shop and they continued to trade here until around 1968. It then became Rees the florist until closure and eventual demolition around the mid 1980s. Also at No.36 Pepper Street, is listed Alfred Newton from 1953 to 1956.

In 1881, at No.38 is listed, Sarah Copestick. There is no further mention of this property number but it is probable that Reynolds' shop incorporated this property, and that it became Riley's Wool Shop from1956 to 1961. It was a fishing tackle shop prior to demolition as previously mentioned around the mid 1980s.

2. 11–27 Pepper Street

It is difficult to place exactly where people lived from the early census returns in this row due to the absence of a numbering system. However, by 1881 the properties were numbered and the occupiers can be listed as follows

No.11   Peter Ashton, Sewing Machine Mechanic
No.13   Benjamin Lloyd, Flour and Provision Dealer
No.15   John Alfred Cartlidge, Butcher
No.17, 19 and 21 all unoccupied
No.23   Henry Cooper, Tailor
No.25   Charles Gould, Boot Upper Fitter
No.27   Frances Hobson, Boot Maker.

In 1935, at No 11 Pepper Street was Harry Stevenson's Fish and Chip Shop. Vaughan mentions the fish and chip shop and a little further on, the local telephone exchange accommodated in the front room of a house. This would be the Post Office Telephone Exchange Ltd., Manageress, Mrs Clayton, listed in the 1913 Directory.

From 1960 to 1972, Acton's Garage and Filling Station is listed at this lower end of Pepper Street. This area is now an open space between modern shops.

3. 16–20 Pepper Street

In 1881, at No.16 Pepper Street was Daniel Mason, insurance agent, and he had a shop for general provisions here in 1896 and 1913. Rupert Bell in his reminiscences, *Old Nantwich*, printed in *Johnsons' Almanacs* in 1931 and reprinted in 1962, remembers him well:

'Passing through Pepper Street, old Daniel Mason will come to the memory of the older generation, a Wesleyan with the quiet ways, retiring manner and the disposition of a Quaker. Daniel Mason eased the bed of sickness and brought peace to many a sorrowing heart, by his kindly benevolence and ready solitude for the dying and the bereaved, many were the funerals he conducted by request.'

In 1935, John Cyril Walsh lived here, at No.16.

In 1881, at No.18 Pepper Street was John Peters, carpenter. He is described as a joiner here in 1896. In 1935 and 1939, James Arden lived here. As there is no mention of either property after this date, it is possible that they were incorporated into the North West Farmers' Shop at No.14 Pepper Street.

In 1881, at No.20 Pepper Street was Thomas Hall, a manufacturer in the boot trade. In 1913, John Meachin, joiner lived here. The following year, he is listed as a bricklayer. In 1935, it was Perrin's Ironmongers Shop and continued in this occupancy until c1957 when it became a shop for the Cheshire Farmers' Association, (to become North Western Farmers' Association in 1959.) It continued as the NWF Shop until at least 1974. Some time after this, the shop closed and the three properties were demolished and replaced with modern shops.

4. 12 Pepper Street

This property was the Wheatsheaf Public House and is so marked on the 1851 Town Map. MacGregor thinks that that it may have opened as the Shepherd's Arms. The licence ran continuously from 1850 to 1911 when it was referred for closure. It closed that same year. MacGregor says:

> 'The report into the condition of the house stated that the house was in a respectable neighbourhood, and that the people who frequented it were "working class". It did very little trade except on a Saturday, the annual turnover being 54 barrels of draught beer. The report also added that the stable for four horses was not used.'

The 1881 census places the Wheatsheaf at No.14 Pepper Street but the 1896 Directory puts it at No.12 Pepper Street. Quite possibly, it occupied both properties at some time.

In 1935, John Basford hairdresser and tobacconist had his shop here. From 1953 to 1955, Hannah Moulton lived here. Some time after this, the building was demolished and a brick wall built between Nos. 10 and 14 Pepper Street. It has now been replaced by modern shops.

5. 9 Pepper Street

Immediately opposite No.12 Pepper Street was No.9 Pepper Street, a double fronted property. This was also a public house but much older than its opposite neighbour. This was the Bluebell, which started as an alehouse whose licence ran continuously from 1769 to 1861. The 1841 census lists Ann Butler as the publican here. MacGregor places Joseph Davies as the licensee here in 1861, but the 1861 census has him at the Wheatsheaf.

In 1871, Thomas Horton, Boot and Shoe Manufacturer, employing 16 men and six women lived here. In 1881 it was unoccupied. By 1896 it had become Gamans and Co. Grocers and Chandlers. Bell has this to say about Gamans around the 1890s or earlier:

> 'A large wholesale grocery business was in full swing at the time of which I write. "Gamans" of Pepper Street., managed by a Mr Blount, a kindly man and a good friend, as the writer can testify. The old tallow candles with which our grandparents were familiar were manufactured here and the fat bought in bulk for the purpose. In that big warehouse were a hundred smells, and methinks a hundred lines of goods, as a whole it almost overcame my youthful and sensitive nostrils – or perhaps I had taken too generously of the of the strong liquorice freely given but not good for the youthful tummy. I recollect their old type round-topped canvas-covered van and pair, being anxiously looked for as 10 or 11 o'clock came on a winter's night; perhaps a heavy fall of snow was the cause of delay. I remember too the great pails of hot mash that so rightly awaited the four-footed wanderers' return.'

In 1913 No.9 Pepper Street had become James Wilson's blacksmith shop. In 1939, Albert Joinson lived here and in 1953 it had become Snape's the haulage contractor. This became Snape's Taxi Service in 1955 and then operating continuously until 1964 when the premises were demolished.

6. 2–6 Pepper Street

No.2/4 Pepper Street was a public house owned by the town of Nantwich and administered through the churchwardens. It started as an alehouse in 1765 and was thought to have been called The Spinning Wheel until 1787 when it became The Ring o' Bells. For a short time in the 1830s it was called The Rising Sun. Its licence ran continuously from 1765 to 1871 when it ceased being a public house and became a Temperance hotel. There is a well-known story of the landlady of this establishment being immortalised in stone. The story goes that stonemasons who were lodging here in the 1850s caught the landlady in the act with her hand in their money pot. At the time, they were renovating the stonework of the Parish Church opposite the premises as part of the Gilbert Scott Renewal Scheme, and so they carved a devil with his hand in a pot of money out of stone and it can be seen high up as a gargoyle in the north west corner of the church exterior.

Bagshaw's Directory of 1850 contains a reference to The Rising Sun which is likely to refer to an earlier date as under the list of hotels and taverns in the same directory it is shown as being The Ring o' Bells.

The Temperance Hotel at the corner of Pepper Street and Churchyardside. Previously it was called The Ring o'Bells in the ownership of Nantwich Town. An upper room was used as The Blue Cap Charity School from 1712 to 1852.

'Harwar's Charity. This property consists of a public-house called The Rising Sun, let at an annual rent of £20, which is distributed as follows:- To the rector, £1. 16s.; the same amount for distribution to the poor; clerk, £1. 16s.; the bellman, 7s.6d.; and to the master of the grammar school, £6. 12s. The residue is added to the weekly bread fund.'

The Blue Cap Charity School was held for many years in an upper room. Apparently it was rented from the Churchwardens, the rental of which was £1 per year in 1713. Funding for the school was from various charities and augmented by gifts from local subscribers, the most notable being the Wilbraham Family. In 1712, 40 boys were being taught and an additional 36 were being taught there in 1836. Every year at this time, each boy was issued with a stout drab jacket, a blue cloth cap, a band, a pair of shoes and a pair of stockings .The money for this was paid by George Wilbraham.

The schoolmasters are listed in Hall and mention must be made of John Thompson or Toby Thompson as he was known. Hall refers to: 'amusing stories being told by old inhabitants of the system of school management and discipline adopted by that old-fashioned and eccentric pedagogue.'

Some recollections of childhood days here between 1837 and 1846 are quite illuminating:

'At some later day I was transferred to a boy's school, in an old fashioned building standing on the edge of the church-yard halfway between the shop and our home, and there learned to read and write under the tutelage of a man to whom the cane was a delight, and who would put a sharp knife under our wrists so that they should not touch the desks while writing. The value of corporal punishment, and the executive ability of a rattan, were usually instilled into us on solemn occasions, in the sanctity of the back room with our breeches down (no chance for protective pads); on less important matters the open hand sufficed; and I doubt not a number of my fellow sufferers can still remember the thrill of delight which ran through the school when the instrument of slaughter had been judiciously split and conveyed some portion of the punishment to the teacher's hand. The building is gone I am told, but the huge oak which nearly covered it, is still there, a memento to the merry throngs who played marbles beneath its shadow and among the tombs.'

Remarkably, Toby Thompson was still teaching here in 1851 at the grand old age of 84 but he did retire in the December of that year. Mr Binns who followed him taught for only six months and then the school closed. It became incorporated into the new Grammar School, which was built in Welsh Row and opened in 1860. According to Hall, the building was pulled down at Christmas in 1879 and a new building erected which became the premises of Mr William Jackson, Draper.

Behind No.6 Pepper Street was a glove factory. In 1792 it was in the ownership of Mrs Hall but occupied by William Hayward. It continued in the possession of the Hayward family until sometime after 1841. In 1851, William Davies had taken over.

Mrs.Isabella Mills in *Threads from the Life of John Mills*, writes to her sister and refers to the gloves made here in 1853:

'... two pairs of useful Nantwich gloves, like those you saw me wearing. They are of a special and famous leather, tanned and made here. Tanning and gloves and shoe-making seem to be the three old staple trades; I bought them from a Mrs Davies, a middle-aged lady, who had a counter half-across the front room of one of the old houses in Pepper Street. Mr Horton says that for nearly 300 years this business has been carried on in the same place; so your gloves have a long pedigree. I say 'a lady' advisedly, for no other term would be correct.'

The glove manufacture ceased in 1863 and the premises became a shoe factory in the possession of George Davenport. The premises fronting the street were probably demolished at the same time as the building next door at Nos. 2 and 4 Pepper Street in 1879. This was replaced with a building of red Ruabon brick.

7. 1–7 Pepper Street

In 1861 at No.1 Pepper Street lived William Lovatt, tailor. In 1871 William Bowker, butcher was living here and in 1881, it was Nathaniel Foxley, flour shop keeper. In 1908, Joseph Hodnett, flour and corn merchant lived here. Vaughan refers to the business:

'After Mr Hodnett's death, the business was managed by his widow and their son Fred. He was a very good-looking young man, one of the heart-throbs of that era. He rode a motorcycle and was travelling along Middlewich Road late one night in August 1917 when he had a bad accident, which later proved to be fatal. It was thought that he may have hit a cow wandering loose on the road, causing him to be thrown and his skull to be fractured. He was very ill for some time at home in Pepper Street and, as was the custom in those days, when the streets were cobbles or setts, a thick layer of tan bark was laid down in the street in front of the shop and for quite a distance on either side to deaden the noise of passing traffic, because on those hard surfaces horses' hooves and wheels of vehicles (which had rims of iron) made a lot of noise.'

By 1935 it had become J H Gibson, Corn Merchant continuing until 1957.

In 1841 at No.3 Pepper Street, was Thomas Smith, publican. This was the Alehouse called The Pig and Whistle and was only open briefly for four years from 1841 to 1844. 'Little' William Dale, tailor lived here in 1871 and 1881 and Mrs Mary Ann Dale, dressmaker. In 1913, Thomas Adams, bootmaker lived here, followed by Arthur Mason in 1935 and 1939. There is no reference to No.3 Pepper Street after that time.

In 1871, at No.5, Pepper Street was John Steventon, Tallow Chandler and Seedsman, employing 2 men, 5 women and 1 boy. In 1881 was Charlotte Jones, Tailor's Machinist, in 1896 was Mrs. Mary Pym and in 1913 was Samuel Walker, Smith. He was still here in 1964.

In 1871, at No.7 Pepper Street was Thomas Horton, Boot and Shoe Manufacturer, employing 16 men and six women. In 1881, there was Thomas Jenkins, tailor, and George Pennington, plumber in 1896; in 1913 it was Thomas Rouse, coach trimmer and in 1935, John Ridgway. There is no reference to No.7 Pepper Street after Elizabeth Ridgway in 1956. It is thought that the whole row of houses from No.1 to 9 Pepper Street were all demolished in 1964 and replaced with a row of modern shops.

8. 1–3 Churchyardside

'A curious old house' is how Hall describes the house of Dr William Wrench, which stood on the site of the present Lloyd's TSB Bank. Hall also refers to the presentation of a sliver medal to Dr Wrench from the Royal Humane Society for restoring to life a boy who had drowned in the canal in 1781. The old house was demolished around 1864 and the new premises for the Manchester and Liverpool District Bank commenced.

The District Bank (as it was called) had previously opened in Barker Street in 1830 then afterwards moved to No.20 High Street, where the manager was Samuel Moore in 1851. It later moved to Mill Street where John Mills was manager from 1852–1864, at what was The Elms. The building then became headquarters for the Liberal Club and is now Peppers Restaurant.

The new Bank in Churchyardside opened in 1866. It also replaced the County Court

Dr. Wrench's old house in Churchyardside. This was demolished when
Stretch and Harlocks was built c1850.

Office that is shown on the 1851 Town Map and was next door to Dr Wrench's house. This building was set back from the street and was fronted by gates with metal railings on each side. The Court was transferred to the new Constabulary in Welsh Row, which had been newly erected in 1860.

The next building towards Pepper Street to be demolished to make way for the Bank was William Lovatt's the draper. He had occupied these premises in 1851.

9. The Midland Bank

In 1871 the census shows Frederick Hobson, manager of the Midland Bank employing seven clerks, occupying the premises. Hall refers to the erection of the Midland Bank on former banking premises in 1876, and the building still stands as the present Barclays Bank. During excavations for the foundations, many coffins were discovered here.

Also on this site previously were James Davies, painter and Jim Bebbington's house and butcher's shop.

10. The Conservative Club

The 1851 census shows that Peter Cumming, tea dealer, may have occupied the premises on what is now the Conservative Club. In 1871 it was John Wright, tea dealer and beer retailer. This building was demolished some time later and the present Conservative Club and Working Men's Club opened in 1881.

11. The Old Grammar School

Immediately opposite what is now the Conservative Club, in the Churchyard stood the Old Grammar School. This half-timbered building was originally built as a Guild Hall but had become a grammar school by 1572, although the foundation of the school is generally accepted as being in 1560. Luckily, the building escaped the fire in 1583, which did so much damage to neighbouring properties.

The school was enlarged in 1611 by the addition of a handsome porch on the south side of the building. The work was carried out by William Dale, Freemason and carpenter, as shown by an inscription on the porch, still legible in 1842. A picture of the porch in the frontispiece of Hall's book shows just how attractive this addition was.

There are few references to work within the school but Edward Lloyd in *Nantwich and Acton Grammar School 1560–1960* quotes a former pupil, The Rev. William Walford, who received his schooling in the 1780s:

'At about nine years of age I was placed at a school in Nantwich, the master of which was a Clergyman, At this seminary I was taught the rudiments of the Latin language and was reading the *Colloquies of Erasmus*, and Ovid's *Metamorphoses*, when I was taken from it... The progress I made in Latin whilst at school has just been now intimated, and was, perhaps, as great as might reasonably be expected,... I subsequently discovered that the instruction given at this school was far from being of the highest order, as may be conceived, when one teacher had to instruct a hundred boys with no other assistance than that of an usher, who attended to writing and arithmetic. The master, who undertook the task of teaching Latin, and in some very few instances Greek, at this school, was very diligent in the performance of his

A pen and ink drawing of The Old Grammar School by Ann Roach. The Old Grammar School was originally The Guild Hall. The school was in continuous use from c1572 to 1858.

daily drudgery; for which, I imagine, he was very insufficiently remunerated. What, however, he could not effect by his diligence, he endeavoured to accomplish by severity. I was not often subjected to the stripes that were every day inflicted, with little discrimination, on the feeble and timid, and on the idle and inattentive, as my lessons were generally prepared in time; and I learned after leaving the school, I was a favourite of the master... The Church Catechism was repeated, in part or entirely, on the Saturdays, and on all the Saints' days we went to the morning prayers of the Church which were often read by our reverend preceptor; and this was always followed by a holiday in the afternoon, as if to reward our extraordinary devotion.'

Lloyd also adds:

'As to the actual number of pupils at the School in the 19th century the Charity Commissioners in 1836 reported that there were eight free boys, fifty day boys and nine boarders. In 1858, when alterations were being made in the churchyard in connection with the restoration of the Church, the old school was demolished and the pupils moved into new buildings in Welsh Row in 1860.'

The Clerk's House is listed in the 1792 Rate Books and according to Hall this was the lower room of the old grammar school; the parish clerk in 1787 and for many years after, being Thomas Cartwright. He was the last to live there. He was followed by Clerk Palin who lived in a house opposite the school. Hall refers to the last band of night watchmen, (and one in particular), who met in the lower room of the grammar school some time around the 1840s:

'In the lower room of the Old Grammar School in the Churchyard, which was then the storehouse of oil, lamps etc. Captain Prince met his men, set their rounds, giving necessary instructions to each for the night; and at the weekend was their paymaster. When the police came, and gas was introduced into the town, the band of watchmen was finally dispensed with; with the exception of Jack Sutton, who continued to be sole night-watchman for High Town, until Christmas 1868, when he was incapacitated by infirmity, and after a protracted illness died Christmas 1870, having been watchman over fifty years. He was a well-known "character" in the town. It was his practice nightly to watch the shops of those tradesmen who gave him a small pittance, (10d. usually) fortnightly, to try their doors; and plaintively cry "parst ten, and a fine starry night;" or otherwise, as the time and weather might be. After which he might be found in some corner or passage of High Street, muffled up in a top-coat, his eyes peering from under an old wide-awake hat, his hands encased in big gloves, and having fixed to his belt a bulls-eye lantern. In these retreats he was always ready to relate how many years it was since he had been in bed at night, or tell of the robberies he had prevented, and his once clever capture of a gang of thieves in Wall Lane; to offer a pinch of snuff, or slyly insinuate that he knew where they were brewing. For many years he had been called "Old Jack Sutton," though he was only 67 years of age at his death.'

12. 21 Churchyardside

The 1871 census shows Henry Bowker, photographer living here. In 1881, he is described as fancy dealer, picture frame maker and photographer. In 1896 and 1913, William Berry, photographer, and picture framer is listed here. In 1939 it is George Berry, radio dealer. In 1959, Betty Ellis has her Ladies' Outfitters Shop with Bert Bebbington the butcher next door. In 1965, William Hatton is listed here but next door is still Bert Bebbington. In 1968 and 1969 is T Hayes Shoe Repairs. There is no reference to No.21 Churchyardside after this time, suggesting that the two shops were demolished around 1970.

13. 23–35 Churchyardside

Bell refers to this group of shops and cottages as follows:

'Another alteration, and, I consider an improvement has been effected by the clearing away of the shops and cottages, once the site of the old Co-operative stores (in Mr Johnny Dutton's time) in the Churchyardside, where the picture house is now erected.'

He mentions two of the inhabitants with some affection, maybe going back to the 1880s:

'One shopkeeper of the old days, known to a wide circle of friends, was the late Edwin Steventon, a seedsman and florist. A man of fine physique and kindly manner; as a very small boy, I recall going to a chapel service held at the workhouse when he preached, and that service remains in my memory nearly fifty years after. One hymn was "Just as I am without one plea," and Edwin led the singing... The late Henry Harding was a townsman in the widest sense, and I write of him as a personal and valued friend. His business premises in the Churchyardside will be remembered, as will his stoneyard and works in Market Street. He was a monumental mason of very high attainments both in wood and stone, he had high ideals in all he was connected with, as with all that he undertook; a highly valued member of the Council for many years, he gave that close attention to its calls that was part of his nature, in Church work he was equally consistent, yet in no narrow sense for no object that was for the welfare of the town appealed or approached him in vain. He made a splendid chairman, his quiet manner, perfect judgement, and impartiality made him to my mind the "ideal". He gave of his wide experience freely. As a member of the Nantwich Debating Society his contributions were always acceptable, reasonable and to the point. His experience of the Continent added greatly to the way in which he so capably described the various forms of architecture and cathedrals of a continental type, Rome, Milan, Venice, Florence. How he interested and instructed. When Henry Harding passed, many including myself, lost a genuine and irreplaceable friend. In latter years he moved his works to the Wellington Road, and his workshop there was always of interest, some piece of sculpture or carving, the details of which he was never too busy to explain to an interested listener.'

At No.23 Churchyardside was Edwin Steventon, at No.25 was Henry Harding , marble mason and the Co-op Stores at No.27 in 1896. In 1913 at No.29 was Miss Williamson, at No.31 was Miss Price, fashionable dressmaker, at No.33 was John Barnett, tanner, and No.35 was Thomas Hobson, engineer.

The Olde Wyche Theatre was built in 1921 and so the shops and cottages were demolished some time before then.

14. The Congregational Chapel School Hall

The Sunday School Hall was built and opened some considerable time after a church meeting authorising the erection of these premises in May 1884. This building was in continuous use until the early 1970s when dry rot had caused severe problems both here and in the chapel next door. Demolition occurred some time after this.

The porch of The Old Grammar School. This was added on to the original building in 1611 by William Dale as shown by an inscription on the porch front.

A view of Churchyardside with the market hall on the right. Just beyond it can be seen Bowkers the photography and picture framing shop.

The Congregational Sunday School in Monks Lane. The Chapel beyond has been converted into apartments.

15. 2–14 Market Street

The 1910 Ordnance Survey Map shows a row of seven cottages that must have been built some time after 1875. The 1913 Directory lists the occupiers as follows:

No.2   John Stenvenson, Seedsman and H. Gentry, Sanitary Inspector
No.4   John Chatwin, Dining Room
No.6   John Wiliamson, Shoemaker
No.8   Charles Williamson, Caretaker
No.10   Thomas Jones, Labourer
No.12   Miss Hassall
No.14   Thomas Hassall

In 1939, at No.4 Market Street was J Chatwin, baker and confectioner, and also Arthur Chatwin. This shows the gradual expansion of Chatwin's Bakery. The cottages continued in private occupation until the mid 1960s, when the Regal Cinema had closed and Chatwin's Bakery began to take over the whole site as it is now.

16. Shoe Factory

Behind the row of houses at 2–14 Market Street was a shoe factory, and in 1913 it may have been Gilbert's Factory although it is listed as being in School Lane.. By 1939 it had become Robinson's Leather Factory. It closed some time later and the buildings have since become absorbed into the Chatwin's Bakery site.

The interior of The Regal Cinema. Taken in the 1930s, this photograph shows the absence of a central gangway. The building has now been amalgamated into Chatwin's Bakery.

17. The Fire Engine House

After a disastrous fire on Snow Hill in 1868, a Volunteer Fire Brigade was formed and a plot of land behind the present market hall was given by Lord Tollemache for the building of a fire station. This building continued to be used for many years after. Simpson takes us back to earlier times when there were two Fire Brigades, and rivalry between them:

'It was not until the 1890s that the Council or Local Board (as it was referred to) Brigade was formed. This being the case two garages were erected side by side in Market Street adjoining the smaller section of the market and immediately facing the Church of England School yard. There were similar doors for each Brigade, the upper half of each being glass panelled. One panel of each covering the bolting handle was of thin plywood so, in case of a fire and upon hearing the "buzzer" (a siren installed at the Gas Works) which gave the alarm any passer-by could smash the panel and release the bolt handle. The doors would then swing open ready for the Firemen to dash in and push out the manual which at the turn of the Century were both hand pumped, and arrive on the Square, where the prancing and excited horses would be waiting for them, supplied from the Crown Hotel Stables (for the Volunteers) and from the stables at Acton Mews, Beam Street (for the Council Brigade). If by chance they were unavailable, horses from nearby Hensons were used... should it be a country fire there would be a thrilling race as to which would arrive first. That of course was when both "engines" were horse drawn. Later when the volunteer engine was motorised the "vols" had a distinct advantage but even then engines could stall and the Council boys would proudly arrive first!... All we boys eagerly looked forward to the "practice nights" held weekly during summer months. "Volunteers" drilled on Tuesday evenings and the "Council" on Thursdays. There would be about twenty of us boys from the Beam Street area perched on the Church of England School wall opposite the Fire Station and we would time them as each fire section ran out their hoses. There were four or six in a section according to the length of hoses ran out. The Captain would blow a whistle at the engine coupling end, then as the nozzle was attached at the target end (which would be the Church) the Sergeant would blow his whistle when the exercise was completed. We onlookers could easily tell the difference between poor or good effort for some of us had watches ourselves to time them with. We all intended to be firemen when we grew up!'

In 1938, the Volunteer Fire Brigade was taken over by the Urban Council and the two brigades amalgamated into one. It was around this time that the Nantwich Fire Brigade moved premises to a new site in Beam Street.

The site in Market Street was taken over by North Western Farmers and later became an egg packing station. More modern premises have been built here and the building, erected in 1992, is known as Pepper House, housing offices for several local businesses.

Nantwich Wholesale Market. This photograph taken c1910 shows the crowded cobbled street, cottages on the right, the two fire engine houses beyond the market hall on the left and the rear of the Market Tavern in the distance at the end of the street.

18. The Baptist Chapel

In 1873, a new Baptist Chapel was built to replace the old one in Barker Street. It had seating for a congregation of 350 people, a good deal larger than the original chapel. In *Dabbers Dissenting*, published in 2003, it is recorded that the church membership in 1874 was 42 and that there had been seven baptisms since the last report. The chapel continued for many years to be a focus for a small but devout congregation. Further interesting insights from *Dabbers Dissenting* are recorded. In the late 1960s, the Congregationalists suggest using their premises for worship as there is concern over the deterioration of their own

The Baptist Chapel in Market Street. This was built in 1873, replacing the old chapel in Barker Street. The cottages to the right were demolished in 1972.

chapel. By 1974 the United Reformed Church, (previously the Congregational Church) had begun worshipping together with the Baptists and sharing activities, and in 1978, the former Congregational Church is sold for redevelopment into apartments. In 1981, the Market

An aerial view from the church looking North. In the lower right is the row of cottages which have now been incorporated into Chatwin's Bakery. Beyond Market Street School is the Civic Hall before alterations to the rear. To the right is the row of houses known as Johnstone's Buildings. Beyond can be seen the Technical Institute and houses in Beam Street.

Street Chapel is demolished but the Victorian school hall behind is retained and refurbished to provide modern facilities for the joint congregation. Several items were transferred from the old chapel, including two sets of windows. These were first presented by Mrs Emma Chatwin in 1955 in memory of her husband (founder of the well known bakery) and a daughter. Mrs Chatwin was a lifelong member of Nantwich Baptist Church from her baptism in 1894. In 1985, the building of Chapel Mews is begun on the site of the former church. The two cottages to the right of the chapel were demolished in 1972, the nearest one to the chapel belonging to the caretaker.

19. Air Raid Shelter

Simpson recalls being an ARP Warden during the Second World War, when temporary accommodation in the form of an extra-sized dug-out (air raid shelter) was built on spare land that is now occupied by the Civic Hall and Library. It could cater for over 300 people, with one main and three smaller exits:

> 'The trouble with it was that it was damp and a pump had to be installed and duckboards covered the ground like an Ypres trench. There were wooden seats all around... I had to pump out the water which covered the duckboards!... amazingly few people took notice of such matters as ARP or other precautions, despite the warnings of Winston Churchill and other top politicians of the danger now at hand.'

There was also an emergency water supply nearby.

20. The Presbyterian Meeting House

Hall refers to the first Meeting House of the Presbyterian Society of Nantwich being in Pepper Street, on the site of cottages belonging to Thomas Johnson of Acton in 1883.

The Nantwich Rate Book of 1691 refers to the property as a malt kiln belonging to Thomas Knutsford and in a deed in 1769 it is referred to in Hall as a 'Warehouse or ancient and decayed piece of Building formerly used as a Meeting-House... and here, the celebrated nonconformist divine, Matthew Henry the son of Philip Henry, who also occasionally visited Nantwich, commenced and finished his remarkable career.'

It would appear that the Meeting House was in use from around 1688 until the Unitarian Chapel was built in Hospital Street and opened in 1726. The 1792 Rate Book shows the only malt kiln to have been at No.7 Pepper Street (or thereabouts) and this could be the possible site.

5 HIGH STREET

1. 2a–2f High Street

On the George Twigg Map of 1624, the area between Waterlode and the River Weaver contains six salt houses along Waterlode and a larger one, owned by Sir Richard Wilbraham, bordering High Street. Behind this salt house is Sir Richard's Garden also known as Lambercotes. This bordered the river from Waterlode to the Town Bridge.

The 1792 Rate Book describes the whole area as house, saltworks and yard adjoining, owned by Mr Hassall. In 1834, Mr Walker was the owner of a saltworks, brine pits, reservoirs, warehouse and weighing machine, and these can be seen on the 1851 Town Map. By 1861, the salt works had closed and Mr Bowker had his second-hand furniture warehouse here. He was still here in 1876. Johnson refers to the site as wasteland, formerly a coal jagger's yard and you can see the coal area clearly on the 1851 Map. The buildings were demolished some time after 1876 and a new row of shops of red Ruabon brick were erected.

Photograph taken in the 1970s of the row of shops at the lower end of High Street just prior to demolition.

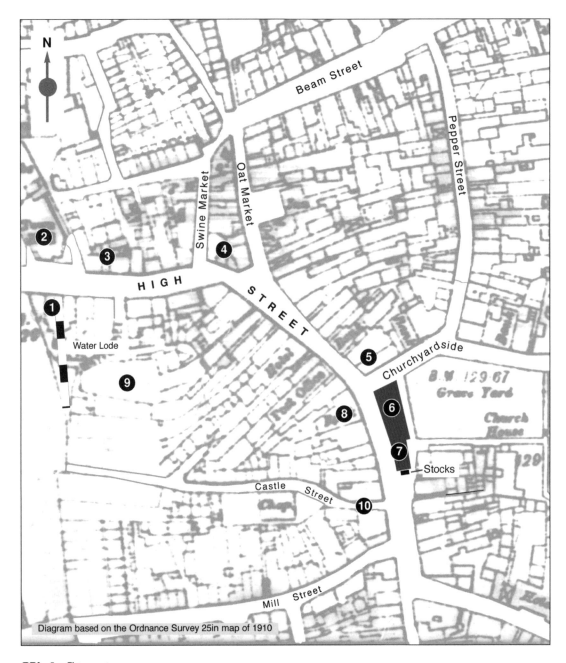

Diagram based on the Ordnance Survey 25in map of 1910

High Street

1 2a-2f High Street
2 The Town Hall
3 1-11 High Street
4 13 High Street
5 31 High Street
6 Old Buildings in The Square
7 Market Hall

8 34-36 High Street
9 Castle
10 Castle Street

In 1892 at No.2 High Street was Edward Rainbow Hill, grocer, and in 1914 was Thomas Cawley, grocer. In 1914, at Nos. 2a and 2b were Charles Edwin Hilditch's boot warehouse, and at No.2c was Mrs Sarah Cawley's Dining Rooms. Vaughan remembers Archie MacKinnon, the well-known artist having a studio above Hilditch's and a window overlooked the river. She also refers to Mill's Fish and Chip Shop with Cawley's Billiard Room upstairs, maybe a door or two further on.

In 1939, at No.2a was I E Cadman, dentist, and Hilditch's boot warehouse was still there. At No.2c was the Electricity Distribution of North Wales Ltd. shop. At No.2d was The Lady Hairdressing Salon, run by E Moseley and at No.2e was Vernon Cooper's radio shop and Melias the Grocers.

By 1953, Nos. 2a, 2b and 2c all had the same owners but at No.2c there was a change of name to the better known one of Manweb. Also at 2c was John Ellson, pork butcher. At No.2d, Flora Peake had her wool shop, and Clifford Kendall, photographer had moved in to 2e, with Melias still on the corner.

In 1964, No.2b had become Norvic Boots and Shoes, but Manweb and John Ellson were still next door at No.2c. Flora Peake was still at No.2d and Clifford Kendall, The Lady Hairdressing Salon and Melias at No.2e.

By 1977, only John Ellson and the Lady Hairdressing Salon were still in operation. Very shortly after this time, the whole row was demolished to make way for the new inner ring road called Waterlode.

2. The Town Hall

A row of buildings consisting of houses and shops are recorded in the 1792 Rate Book on the site of the Town Hall. These had all been demolished by 1851 and the site was waste ground. In 1858 a new Town Hall was erected by public subscription at a cost of £2,500. In 1868, due to insecure foundations, it was partly dismantled and rebuilt at a cost exceeding £1,050. It incorporated a corn exchange, committee Rooms for the use of the Local Board, the Volunteer Rifle Company Armoury and Drill room and an assembly room which could seat 1,000 people. The hall was used regularly for concerts with many touring companies using the building. It was later used for magic lantern shows and silent films. Both Vaughan and Simpson give anecdotes of activities here. It was also used for public meetings and elections, and later, dances were held regularly here up until 1939.

In 1883 at the rear of the Town Hall was built a brine swimming pool and medicinal baths. Simpson remembers it well. The baths were approx. 20 yards by 8 yards with a depth from 3 to 6 feet. He was taught to swim during school time by Mr H C Barker from the National School in Market Street, 'bath day' being on a Tuesday. Some mothers refused to allow their children to go for swimming lessons. One lady sent a note which read 'I don't want our Walter to go to the baths until he can swim'!

The brine, supplied from the brine spring on site, pumped into the baths, was soothing and refreshing and aided buoyancy. There were also private baths behind for sufferers of rheumatism and a pail of brine to bathe with could be bought for sixpence.

In 1945, the building was considered unsafe for public meetings and was converted into a store for motor accessories. This firm failed and it was later let to Bill Spode for a timber and DIY Store. It had become empty by 1965 when the rest of Snowhill was swept away, and eventually demolished in 1972 to make way for an entrance to the Snowhill Car Park.

Photograph looking up High Street from Welsh Row. The tower of the Town Hall can be seen on the left. The tower was demolished for safety reasons.

Nantwich town bridge with the Town Hall on the right. The chimney belongs to the old brine baths.

A view of the lower end of High Street looking towards Welsh Row. Cawley's Tearooms can be seen on the left, the Town Hall restaurant on the right. This building was previously The Market Tavern.

Howard's clothing shop at No 1 High Street photographed in 1961. It is the same building as the one on the right of the previous picture.

3. 1–11 High Street

In 1792, at No.1 High Street, was the Horse and Jockey Public House, the licensee being widow Jones. It may originally have been called the Horse and Groom. By 1796 it had become the Bridge Tavern and its licence ran continuously until closure in 1892. In 1876 its licensee was Billy Gilbert as remembered by Johnson, and its owners were John and W W Downes who also owned Nos. 3 and 5 High Street. In unpublished work, David and Doreen Mason give details of the Bridge Tavern in 1891. Its owner was W W Downes, banker. Its licensee was Edward Mason who resided on the premises. It was a free house, i.e. not tied to a brewery. It had eight beds for travellers and accommodation to supply refreshments for 16 persons. There were three stables and three stalls for horses. Its back entrance was in another street used by the public (probably in Snow Hill). The overall remarks were 'a good house and good accommodation' and yet it closed just one year later.

In 1896, the Town Hall cocoa rooms, run by William Mottram, are listed here. By 1939 they had become Howard's Outfitters and Draper's Shop and continued in their possession until demolition c1960.

At No.3 High Street in 1876 was Martha Davies and in 1896, Edwin Bayliss, cabinet-maker. By 1913 it had become Hulse's Cycle Stores. In 1953, Cliff Morse's cycle shop was here until demolition c1960.

At No.5 High Street in 1876, was Thomas Bolton, shoe manufacturer, and in 1896 was Joseph Barnett, painter, plumber and sign-writer. He was still here in 1913, but by 1939, it had been taken over by Hulse's Cycle Shop.

At No.7 High Street in 1876 was John Taylor, hatter, and in 1896 was Mrs. Sophia Kinsey, ladies' outfitter. In 1913 it had become Cawley and Perrin's, Ironmongers, but in 1939 and 1953, it was Preston and Day's, Gent's Outfitters. In the early 1960's it belonged to Bill Schofield before being demolished with the other buildings in this row.

At No.9 High Street in 1876 was Lucy Worsey, confectioner. It continued trading as Worsey's for many years until closure in the early 1960s. There was a café behind the shop in 1939 and later. In *A Boy's Eye View of Nantwich* in 1922, by T W Freeman, written in *Johnson's Almanac*, Worsey's shop is mentioned:

Cliff Morse's cycle shop at No.3 High Street.

> 'Worsey's was a shop much admired for its wonderful cakes and delectable pork pies, and particularly for its bath buns. The shop had an old-fashioned air with a glade of ferns in one corner; and fascinating brandy snaps were stored in large glass jars. It was presided over by a tiny lady whose dresses swept the floor, Mrs Hallmark, who was said to view followers of her assistants with little favour. She was immensely competent as a caterer, and provided tea for the vast Methodist gatherings of the day in fierce competition with the jovial Mr Picken of the Cocoa House, next to the Library.'

Schofield's clothing shop at Nos 5 and 7 High Street.

An article in the *Nantwich Chronicle* in 1952 gives some interesting information on the property. Apparently the bakery business here was founded in 1780 and an original hoist which was used to lift heavy bags of flour was still in use in 1952. The business came into the possession of Sampson Cartwright in the early 1800s and later was owned by Mrs Worsey. She then passed it on to her son Sampson Cartwright Worsey who later became the general manager of The Brine Baths Hotel. Not many people know that behind the shop was a hidden street called Cricket Street and the cobblestones between the shop and bakehouse were still there in 1952.

At No.11 High Street in 1876 was Anthony Carrington's newsagent's shop, and by 1896 it had become Henry J Carrington's stationer's shop. It 1913, Miss Carrie Carrington had taken over the stationer's shop, and in 1939, Carrington's newsagent's shop was in the hands of E White, proprietor. For a short time it was also the *Nantwich Chronicle* Office. The author remembers descending two steps into the shop and the counter was along the length of the shop but the room was not very deep from front to back.

Worsey's bakery, confectioner's shop and café at No 9 High Street. The business was established in 1780 by Samuel Cartwright, miller and baker.

Carrington's newsagent's shop at No 11 High Street. Many people remember the step down into the shop on entering.

4. 13 High Street

The buildings on the island site facing High Street are of interest. According to Johnson the first shop was Hulse the saddler's with Jonathan Kitchen's butcher's shop adjoining. In 1876 the building was owned by the Marquis of Cholmondeley. To enter the shop from the Swine Market side you had to climb three steps. In 1896 it was in the possession of Egerton C Gilbert, tobacconist and in 1913 it was Joseph C Gilbert, tobacconist. In 1939, it still traded as Gilbert's but the Proprietor was L G Odd. In 1953 it was Finlay's tobacconists and continued in their possession until demolition of the island site in the mid 1960s.

The next shop looking up towards the Square was Mrs Carrington's hat shop. Johnson refers to it: 'Down two steps into her old shop, filled with hat boxes containing beaver hats and bonnets of a past age; she was over 90 years of age.'

In 1913 at No.13a was James B Withington, confectioner, at No.13b was James Smith and Son, dyers, and at No.13c was Robert Dixon, grocer. There was an office for the Overseer of the Poor above Dixon's store around this time. In 1939, this building had become the Zan Stores, proprietor, John Baines, continuing as the Zan Stores until eventual closure before demolition in the mid 1960s.

Johnson's shop in High Street, now part of Peter Williams the chemist.

Looking up High Street towards Gilbert's tobacconists and the Zan hardware stores.

A similar view to above.

High Street looking towards Oat Market. Dixon's shop can be seen on the Oat Market/Swine Market site. Note the granite sets in the street.

5. No.31 High Street

In 1834, Richard Stretch of Messrs R and J Stretch owned the property and had a draper's shop here, which was previously in the ownership of Robert Butters. Judy St Pourcain (née Stretch) has researched extensively into the partnership of the well-known Nantwich firm of Stretch and Harlocks. Her unpublished work provides fascinating information surrounding the building of the new shop premises on this site, with first a description of the old shop:

'The shop which Joseph (Stretch) inherited from his father (Richard) was of brick with a rounded front window of small panes of glass. The door was cut in two – like a stable door – with a bell on it to announce the entrance of a customer.

The interior was of a good size with a low ceiling. The shop was separated from the counting house or office in the rear by a door which led into a narrow tile-floored passage leading to a few cramped rooms and a tiny back yard, more rooms being upstairs.

In 1859 Samuel Harlock's business had grown so much he was contemplating a new building to take the place of the old structure which had housed the family business for so many years.

Meanwhile Richard Stretch had continued with his architectural studies and he drew up plans for the new building. It was to be a three-storey and basement brick building faced with stone covering an irregular plot of ground facing High Street. The plan was to buy some adjoining properties and demolish them together with their own shop and replace them with a building some 50 to 60 feet by 100 to 120 feet in area. One of the properties would not be available until June (could this be Dr Wrench's old house? ed.) so Richard decided to go to America for the year to visit his Uncle Jesse Stretch who was a farmer out there.

A year later in 1860 Richard returned to Nantwich to oversee the building of the new shop and to see the plans he had drawn up bear fruit.

Firstly the old brick built shop had to be demolished although it was probably a hundred years younger than the adjoining properties which were also to go; it fell

Stretch and Harlock's old shop on the corner of
High Street and Churchyardside.

easily but when it came to the demolition of the other properties which appeared from the street to be ready to fall if they were pushed it was a different proposition altogether. After removing the brick mortar and rubble filling of the big timber framework they found that the oak frame was as sound as when it was first put into place. The framework was put together with mortise and tenon joints and oak pins. Each one had to be removed with infinite labour. There was not one nail in the whole framework.

Even more surprises were to await them. When the digging of the foundations was begun, the discoveries were astonishing.

About two feet down they unearthed a portion of old cobblestone pavement with burnt straw and a kitchen midden or cesspool complete with chicken bones and egg shells. About six feet down they found that the shop had been built on part of the old cemetery, as human bones were abundant. They also found part of the foundations of some building of an earlier date. At ten feet they came to the original sandy soil with a few oak beams, black as ink and soft enough to cut easily but which became as hard as iron after exposure to the air for a short time. All the material taken from the excavation was carted away for manure. It contained bones of oxen, sheep, goats, deer and pigs.'

There is also a reference to the site, of interest, in Hall:

'Old people now (1883) living remember an open shop that stood in the centre of the town, on the site of handsome premises now occupied by Mr S Harlock, where Mr E Barrowcliffe, butcher, *killed* and *dressed* his meat, before exposing it for sale.'

6. Old Buildings in the Square

The 1792 Rate Book describes 6 properties in this island site as follows:

Part of Dr Gardner's Shop, Parlour, Surgery and Wash House
Butcher's Shop, Part of Dr Gardner's Shop, Kitchen and small Outlet
Part of a Shop and other part as Warehouse, owned by Peter Walthall
House and Shop, owned and occupied by Messrs Cliffs
House and Shop, occupied by William Fox.
In 1834, (a) was empty; in (b) was Widow Bebbington's butcher's shop with Mr Walton's Auction Rooms; (c,d and e) were occupied by Messrs J and G Cliffe; and (f) was occupied by Miss Tilsley.
In the 1841 census, Mary Tilsley is described as a tea dealer, Joseph Cliff is an upholsterer, next door is Anthony Merga, watchmaker, and finally Anne Cornes, innkeeper's wife.
In the 1851 census are possibly, Gilbert Murray, draper; Mary Abrahams, hardware shop; James Hargreaves, draper's assistant; Joseph Thomas, grocer and W Levinson, tailor.
In the 1861 census are Lucy Merga's toy shop and Frederick Smith, draper.
In the 1871 census are only Bowyer, hairdresser and Walley, draper. Willett remembers Billy Bowyer having his hairdresser's shop here.
In 1872, these buildings were demolished and an open space created which is now known as the Square.

The rear of the old shops on the Square before demolition in 1872
with the church graveyard in the foreground.

7. The Market Hall

There are two references to the Booth Hall or Court House in *The Place Names of Cheshire, Part 3,* by J McNeil Dodgson. The first is in Cholmondeley Papers in 1579 and the second reference in Ormerod's *History of Cheshire.* The Booth Hall is given as 'a great hall in which Assizes are held, a town hall.'

In Hall, there is more detail on later buildings. A Market Hall was erected in 1720 with a Sessions Room above. The then Prince of Wales, (later King George the Second) gave £600 towards the building and an effigy of him ornamented the south side of the building. In 1737, at about six o'clock in the evening on Saturday the 14 May, the building fell down and nine people were killed. Some of their names are listed in Hall. The gritstone effigy broke in half and its upper part can still be seen locally. Only 22 years later, in 1759 a sudden crash during a Quarter Sessions alarmed the Court and many were hurt in the stampede to get out of the building quickly. Due to safety concerns, Quarter Sessions were transferred to Knutsford in 1760, the upper room taken down and the lower part retained as a market place for farmer's wives who would bring their baskets of butter, eggs, poultry and provisions to sell.

> 'This Market Hall, which met with the requirements of the town until 1868, was a low building in the High Town, opposite Castle Street. Its roof was supported by brickwork on semicircular arches that rested on nine granite columns; the only ornament being a plume of feathers (the badge of the Prince of Wales) on the cornice above the central pillar on the south side.'

There is reference to a new 'cage' (probably a temporary prison) being erected near the site of the old Market Hall in 1592. Thomas Church, living at 46 High Street, (now Nantwich Bookshop) refers to a 'room next the cage ' in his will and inventory of 1635. This cage could therefore have been situated on the south end of the building particularly as a pair of stocks can be seen in this position on the 1851 Town Map.

As previously stated, the Market Hall was demolished in 1868, but the adjoining properties were still left standing until 1872 when they were taken down.

8. 34/36 High Street

On the site of the present Natwest Bank used to stand Parr's Bank, but before it was built there were two separate properties here. In 1851, at No.34 High Street was George Harrison, fruit and confectionery dealer and next door at No.36 was Anthony Merga, watchmaker and toyshop. In 1861, at No.34 was Mary Harrison, fruit and confectionery dealer and next door at No.36 was George Lewis, confectionery dealer.

In 1876, George Lewis owned both properties. At No.34 was still Mary Harrison, but she was now selling fancy goods and fruit. Next door was Miss Bird, milliner. Willett remembers Mrs. Harrison:

'The first place I visualise is the little toyshop and servant's registry office next door to Harry Poole, the watchmaker, and facing the shop of Billy Bowyer the barber, before that block of shops and the market hall were taken down. Mrs Harrison, an ancient dame, was the tenant, and what a treat it was to me (then under eight years of age) to help her unpack her case of toys and to receive as a reward a nice juicy orange! For you must remember that oranges at that time (now available all the year round) were only in season for about a month or so and all I had to spend at the weekend was my "market penny." '

In 1892, at No.34 was Miss Esther Charlesworth, dressmaker and at No.36 was Mrs Selina Spence, dressmaker. In 1896, at No.34 was John Chesters, butcher and at No.36 was Miss Frances Jackson, confectioner.

Some time after this, the buildings were demolished and Parr's Bank erected on this site. This building continued as Parr's Bank until some time before 1939 when it had become The National Westminster Bank. Natwest continued using this same building until the 1980s, when it was replaced with the present modern structure on the same site.

9. Nantwich Castle

Although direct evidence of a castle at Nantwich is almost non-existent, there are pointers to its whereabouts. Castle Lane still exists now as a narrow alleyway leading from the High Street to the riverside. The castle was probably built by William Malbank around 1100A.D. It is mentioned in 1288 when it is thought that Sir John Lovell purchased it from the Malbank family.

An archaelogical dig was carried out in this area in 1978 and signs of a ditch around the castle mound were found. Robina McNeil Sale in her report of that year, 'The Crown Car Park Excavations' has this to say:

'The castle was likely to have been sited in a commanding position. The ideal spot is under the Crown Hotel and Densems clothes shop (now P Williams, Chemists) where the ground rises from the river to this point. This particular spot is one of the few higher areas in Nantwich, commanding an excellent position for the river and the hinterland behind.'

It is said that some sandstone blocks originating from the old castle were re-used in the building of St Mary's Parish Church.

Parr's Bank. This has been replaced by the modern Natwest Bank on the square. Note the granite setts on the road.

10. Castle Street

In 1792 the Rate Book named Castle Street as Pudding Lane. This was in reference to butcher's stalls being in the vicinity and the lane being used to dispose of the offal (probably in the river!). Certainly Mr Edward Barrowcliffe had a slaughterhouse here. There are 16 properties listed of which six were houses, eight were stables and there was a flax dresser's and nailer's shop and the slaughterhouse previously mentioned.

By far the most interesting properties are the ones known as Castle House. According to Hall, the apprentices of Bott's Mill lived in a large airy house that stood on the site of the Ebenezer Chapel in Castle Street. This would be the property described in the Rate Book as House, Yard, Garden and Stable, owned by Mr Stretch and occupied by Messers Stretch and Newton in 1792. In 1833 it was owned by Mr Richards and Mr Walton and occupied by Mr Dereimer and Samuel Sumner.

In 1835 the Wesleyan Methodist Association was formed by some dissenters of the Wesleyan Chapel in Hospital Street .At first they worshiped in a school-room in Pall Mall but later purchased the Castle House, fitting it up as a chapel and calling it The Tabernacle. The 1851 Map shows the outline of the building. In 1857, it was pulled down and the Ebenezer Chapel, seating 120 persons, erected on the same site. In 1874 it had become The United Methodist Free Church and the Minister was Rev. J Dent. In 1896 it had no resident Minister.

By 1913, the United Methodist Church had moved to Pillory Street and the building had become the Picturedrome and later the Cosy Cinema. In 1968 it had become The Birdcage Club, The Wayfarer Club in 1971, Roosters in 1974 and now is Gregory's Night Club.

Next door, between the Old Vaults and the above-mentioned building, also in Castle House according to Hall, lived Miss Elizabeth Webb, a wealthy maiden lady. She is listed as living here in 1792 but had died by March 1828, aged 83. Apparently she had in her possession a tortoiseshell knife and fork that had once belonged to Mrs Elizabeth Milton, wife of the famous poet John Milton.

Johnson refers to some properties in Castle Street as follows:

'Some of the cottages here were of a very decrepit character, tenanted by the poor Irish of the town. At Harvest Time, Irish labourers lodged there. These men came over to assist the farmers and earn sufficient to pay their rent. On Saturday nights there were frequent "disagreements" in Castle Street, not always the fault of the visitors from Ireland.'

Bell gives us a portrait of a real Nantwich 'character' Tommy Fiddler here:

'I well remember on one occasion, a constable of huge physique, named Scott, disturbing Fiddler's dreams, after imbibing not wisely, but too well on the steps of the old Ebenezer Chapel in Castle Street. Tommy took it in quite good part, but refused to either get up or walk; the constable used every fair method but Fiddler continued to roll over, and get back to the starting point; ducking and dodging, feinting as if to fight his tall adversary, and again running a few yards, when, drawn up to his full height, he would march again to his original resting place. The few onlookers saw a mirth in the grotesque incident that the constable did not share, and eventually he was pushed and partly carried into the square. Just when he appeared to be going quietly, probably having promised to do so, he broke away again, and the constable proceeded to handcuff him, but Tommy lay on his back, hands thrust deep in his trousers' pockets, and the massive arm of the Law standing over him, first pulling out one hand and then the other. Fiddler seemed to enjoy it for he ejaculated in a sufficiently loud voice to be heard "Eh! What fun we're 'avin," in that nasal drawl of his that small boys of his period loved to mock – at a respectful distance. I believe Thomas was, in the end, ignominiously placed upon a handcart as the easiest method of terminating his 'five-foot-four of fun.'

Willett also has this to say about Tommy Fiddler:

'Tommy Fiddler! Poor old Tommy! Of all the dirty, dishevelled, idle yet lovable characters, Fiddler would be hard to beat. My contemporaries need no pen picture of Thomas, but for record's sake and the younger generation he is worthy of a character sketch. Thomas was very short of stature, had dark rather merry eyes, an insignificant dab of a nose, and oftener than not long dishevelled hair and beard sprinkled with grey and of medium length. Always his hair needed cutting and often hid the dirty red scarf he wore tied in a sailor's knot fashion. His clothes varied, save for a consistency of misfit, from a small tight coat and wide over-long trousers, "concertina'd" rather than creased, to an over-large coat of the tail fashion that almost clothed him in itself; or again, a rag of a coat, that showed between gaps remnants of lingeries, now buttoned up tightly, now drawn together in a vain attempt to meet with the aid of string and safety pins. Fiddler's hats, like a famous politician's, varied from a hard felt, from which the crown was obviously parting company, to a soft cap a size too large for him. He wore them well pulled down over his narrow forehead. Fiddler had a peculiar gait, often it became a march in caricature, a long stride with short legs, and a bearing of a semi-military character, but always or almost invariably, Thomas was good tempered and of a humorous nature. One remarkable feature of Fiddler was to dispense with attache case or handbag and carry his very personal belongings inside his hat. This being known to the precocious of the day, it was quite fun in their estimation to, dislodge Fiddler's hat; and many times this has happened with the sequel that Tommy was down on his knees, eloquent with threats, emitting curses to all and sundry as he regained his precious assortment of odd matches, pins, rags, buttons, broken bits of comb, and miscellany.'

The first Nantwich to Crewe Omnibus on the square in 1905. In the middle of the picture is the Printing Office that was converted soon after to what we now know as W.H.Smiths newsagent and bookshop.

Castle Street looking towards the square. The side of No.46 High Street, now Nantwich Bookshop is in the middle of the picture.

6 MILL STREET, BARKER STREET

1. Johnson's Court

It is difficult to identify the houses here in the 1792 Rate Books and the 1851 Town Map indicates that there may have been four cottages here. Johnson refers to two cottages here in Mill Street. '25 yards down on the right was an entry to an open yard, paved with cobblestones in front of two decrepit cottages; in the centre of this yard, a post with tap and grid beneath which served the cottages.'

2. 20–34 Mill Street

There was a row of cottages on the north side of Mill Street stretching down to Bower's Row. There was a gap in the row between Nos. 24 and 26 to allow access to the timber yard behind Nos. 26–34 in 1851. There were also narrow entries between Nos. 20 and 22 and Nos. 30 and 32 shown on the same map.

The timber merchant at the timber yard and cottages was William Ikin in 1822. In 1833 he is listed as a joiner.

3. Cotton Factory and Waterworks

According to Hall, waterworks were erected immediately after the fire of 1583 and built on the north side of the corn mills at the end of Mill Street by the river. Hollowed out logs were laid end to end in the principal streets with fire plug connections at intervals. Water was raised from the river by means of a wheel.

On the same site, a cotton mill was established here around 1785 in a building next to the river. In 1792 it was owned by Edleston and Co. and managed by Ralph Fogg, cotton master of Manchester. It was known locally as Fogg's Mill. In 1799 a fire destroyed both cotton factory and waterworks, the ruins are said to lie in the bed of the river.

4. Bower's Row

Some time later a row of cottages was built on the same site, with gardens stretching down to the river, to house workers at the other cotton mill next door. This terrace was named Bower's Row after Thomas Bower who had bought the mill from the previous owner, Richard Bott.

In 1833, there were eight tenants in the row, each paying a 5d annual rate. In 1896, there were 10 tenants. The cottages were in continuous occupation until 1970 when they were pulled down.

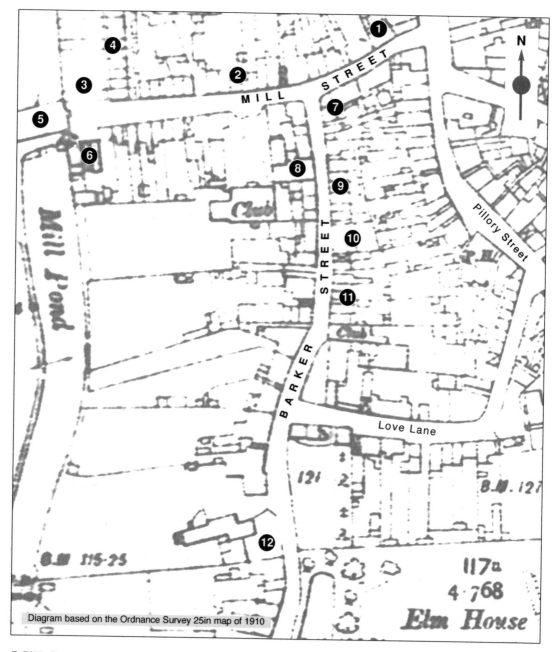

Diagram based on the Ordnance Survey 25in map of 1910

Mill Street, Barker Street

1 Johnson s Court
2 20-34 Mill Street
3 Cotton factory and Waterworks
4 Bowers Row
5 Nantwich Corn Mill
6 Cotton twist warehouse
7 1 Barker Street

8 2-10 Barker Street
9 15 Barker Street
10 The Baptist Chapel
11 17-25 Barker Street
12 24-32 Barker Street

5. Nantwich Corn Mill

The earliest reference to a corn mill in Nantwich is in 1228 and Manorial Rights were exercised by the various lords of the Manor. It came into the possession of Robert Cholmondeley, Baron of Wich Malbank around 1650 and continued in the same family until 1840 when it was sold by George, second Marquis of Cholmondeley to Messrs Bower and Co. According to Hall, about 1789 it changed to a cotton spinning factory under Messrs Birch, Randles and Bower, Michael Bott becoming a partner in 1790. In 1797, the mill was enlarged and steam machinery added, mainly through the enterprise of Mr Bott. It became known afterwards as Bott's Mill.

There is an interesting article on the history of cotton manufacture in Nantwich by W H Chaloner, which was printed in *Johnson's Almanac* in 1938 and this covers the period from 1789 at this mill until the cotton mill closed down in June 1874. The building was raised to its full height and new machinery added when Thomas Bower succeeded his father and was joined by two partners by the name of Lowe in 1840.

The mill was purchased by John Whittingham of Batherton Mill in 1874 and used again as a corn mill. He also had an iron foundry and made cast iron cheese presses. Johnson says that he was more interested in machinery than corn milling and he purchased the first steam roller in the district.

Bell refers to this area:

> 'Mill Street was one of the Town's industrial workshops in these past days, in Whittingham's yard might be seen above the fencing, funnel after funnel, tractors, and all the tackle associated with engineering and threshing business, while next door were the coach and iron works of Henry Shakeshaft's earlier days; the flour mills of Mr Batho, and for a period at least a fustian works and a clothing works.'

In 1939, Thomas Batho was still here with part of the building being used as a billiard hall. The mill was destroyed by fire in 1970 and subsequently demolished.

Nantwich Mill. View from the town bridge.

Nantwich Mill at the lower end of Mill Street showing the office and saleroom of John Boughey.

Nantwich Mill facing the mill leat and sluice-gate. Note the number of tie bars used to secure the walls.

Nantwich Fustian Mill at the rear of the previous picture. Fustian was a material similar to corduroy and used for work clothes.

Interior of Nantwich Mill showing sacks of animal feed.

6. Cotton Twist Warehouse

The 1851 map shows a cotton twist warehouse situated on the side of the river bank to the south of the corn mill. It had a central covered entry and there were three small cottages behind. It was used for the storage of cotton twist, or yarn as it is more commonly called nowadays. This was the finished product from the cotton mill. There is no trace of the building now.

7. 1 Barker Street

Hall suggests that this may have been The Butcher's Arms once and the adjoining properties to have been a butcher's row (shambles) but does not indicate when. It could have some connection with the Wickstead Arms, which is on that same corner of Mill Street and Barker Street. The 1851 Town Map shows no building here. In 1896, the property was inhabited by Mrs Sarah Jones, but by 1913 it had been demolished.

8. 2,4,6,10 Barker Street

The 1792 Rate Book shows a small dwelling house and malt kiln here, owned by Joseph Jackson. They can be seen on the 1851 Town Map. In 1896, 2, 4 and 10 were inhabited next to Hobson's Shoe Factory. In 1913 and 1939, both Nos. 6 and 10 were lived in but had gone by 1953.

9. 15 Barker Street

In 1896, William Broomhall, gardener, lived here. It was then in continuous occupation until some time after 1977 when it was demolished.

10. The Baptist Chapel

In 1725 a single storey brick building was built here some way from the street to accommodate Nantwich's first Baptist Society. In front of the building, raised above road level was a small burial ground believed to be the last resting place of Alice Milton, third wife of the famous poet John Milton, who died in 1727.

The first Baptist Minister was Samuel Acton who lived at The Elms in Mill Street (later the District Bank, then the Liberal Club and now Pepper's Restaurant.). He supervised the building of the Chapel and it is thought that hw was also buried in the graveyard there.

In 1772, the Baptist cause fell on hard times and the Chapel closed. In 1777, the Trustees leased the chapel to the local Methodist Society and John Wesley preached here three times, in April 1779, March 1780 and May 1781. The Chapel was used continuously by the Methodists until 1808 when they moved to their new premises in Hospital Street.

Around 1812, the Baptist cause was revived by a eight people and local shoemaker, John Cooper took pastoral charge. It appears that there

The old Baptist Chapel in Barker Street. It was shut for forty years and when reopened in 1862, grass was growing through the floor and almost to the tops of the pews.

was some disagreement among the Trustees around this time as one of them had allowed the use of the building by another denomination. It is said that the Reverend John Cooper, locked the chapel door and left the town. It stayed closed for 40 years.

The Chapel re-opened on 27 April 1862. They had to break open the door to gain entry, and the first service was held with grass growing through the floor and reaching almost to the tops of the pews. It was extensively renovated and repaired and an official re-opening of the renovated chapel was held on 21 May 1865. The Baptist Society later moved to its new premises in Market Street in 1873 and the old chapel was sold to the Order of Good Templars. It later became a meeting place for the Salvation Army. During the Second World War it was used regularly for youth meetings by the Salvation Army. Afterwards it was used as a baker's warehouse. It was finally demolished in October 1957.

11. 17–25 Barker Street

A row of cottages stood here, some of them black and white. At No.21 Barker Street in 1896 was John Weston, lodging-house keeper. He is also listed as a lodging-house keeper, opposite, at No.32 Barker Street, that same year. In 1913, Mrs A Weston is living here but is not listed as a lodging-house keeper, suggesting that the building was no longer a lodging-house.

By 1939, No.17 Barker Street had been demolished and No.25 may have been used as Urban Council Offices. Some time before 1953, Nos. 19 to 23 Barker Street were demolished, and the site is now a car park for the local firm of solicitors of Hibberd, Durrad, Moxon.

12. 24–32 Barker Street

Hall suggests that Cheney Hall occupied, or was near this site. There was certainly a barn belonging to Cheney Hall opposite the building in Love Lane that was pulled down in 1788 and two almshouses erected on its site.

The 1851 Town Map shows a large malt house, a smaller one, a malt kiln and a brewhouse to the south of the building known for many years as the Dowery at No.22 Barker Street. The 1792 Rate Books describe the property as Messers Walley's house, yard, garden and stable, a large malt kiln and a small malt kiln, all in the occupation of Samuel Barker.

The next property is described in the same year as Messrs Barker and Wrench, house, garden and stable in the occupation of Mrs Dutton, and these can be clearly seen on the 1851 Town Map.

Adjoining this house is Mr James Tunstall's thread shops and garden at back. The thread shops may refer to the production of cotton thread perhaps on a small-scale basis. The *Cowdroy Directory* of 1789 shows that John and Richard Tomlinson had a threadmaking business in Barker Street and it must have been here. Oddly enough James Tunstall is listed as a painter. The 1851 Town Map does show two small properties here which could be the thread shops referred to above. In 1833 they are described as house and yard and Mr Tunstall pays. This would be Croudson Tunstall who is listed as a thread manufacturer in Barker Street in *Pigot's 1822/3 Directory*.

The next building is described in 1792 as Mr Tunstall, house and garden, and garden adjoining and in the occupation of James Tunstall. In 1833 it was owned by Mr Croudson Tunstall and the occupier was John Beck.

In 1896, there was a lodging-house at No.32 Barker Street, kept by John Weston and Mrs A Weston was the lodging-house keeper in 1913. By 1939 it had ceased to be a lodging-house.

No.24 Barker Street is not mentioned in directories after 1939 and so °may have been demolished. However, the other properties continued in existence until at least 1977 when the last directory of Nantwich was published. Some time fairly soon after this, the other houses were demolished to make way for the present Waterlode inner ring road. No.34 Barker Street still exists but is separated from the rest of Barker Street by the above mentioned road.

Old black and white cottages in Barker Street.

The same view today. The building on the right can be identified from the previous picture.

7 PILLORY STREET, LOVE LANE

1. 3–7 Pillory Street

At No.3 Pillory Street was an alehouse which, in 1782 was called The Coach and Horses. Around 1793, it was The Shoulder of Mutton, under which sign it existed until 1826 when it became The Albion. In 1834 it changed its name to The Golden Lion and continued with that name until closure in 1894. According to MacGregor, it was leased to the Congleton Brewery Co. in 1891. In 1894 it had closed for want of a tenant. The licensing magistrates refused to renew its licence, saying that the house was small and there was a good fully-licensed house next door. The building stood empty for several years before being pulled down with adjoining properties in 1910.

At No.5 Pillory Street was an inn called The George and Dragon that was a free house for all the years of its existence. It opened in 1767 and closed around 1906. It was commonly known as The George in the early 1800s. In 1841, it was known as The Green Dragon for a short while before reverting to its original name. The later landlords were Francis Jubb from 1871 to 1883, Annie Jubb from 1887 to 1888, John Cornes in 1890 and 1906 and Annie Cornes from 1891 to 1903. It may be that at some time the George acquired the premises next door at No.7 Pillory Street. The building was demolished along with its neighbouring property in 1910.

At No.7 Pillory Street was another alehouse for a short while. This was The Blue Barrel, owned by Wilbraham Tollemache and its licence ran from 1773 to 1792 when it closed. In 1833, it was owned by Admiral Tollemache and occupied by George Boughey, being described as a house and old back buildings. By 1861 it was in the occupation of John Parker, painter and plumber, employing one man and three assistants. He was still there in 1881, but was now described as a plumber and plasterer. In 1896, Thomas Parker, painter was living here, perhaps he was the son of John Parker. Somewhere around this time the house was demolished and the present building which now houses a menswear shop was erected.

2. 1–7 Love Lane

The 1851 Town Map shows a row of cottages along the south side of Love Lane stretching from the end of Pillory Street to the corner of what is now the entrance to a car park. A total of 12 cottages can be counted on the map. There is no other direct reference to them and they may have been converted to other uses when the houses were numbered in the mid-1870s. The corner shop in Pillory Street, an antiques shop further along the street and a garage at the far end now occupies this site.

3. Meakin and Delves Almshouses

In 1788, a barn belonging to Cheney Hall was pulled down and two almshouses erected on the same site. A further four almshouses were also built with the charity money arising from the bequests of Mrs Ermine Delves in 1722 and Matthew Meakin in 1738. These almshouses

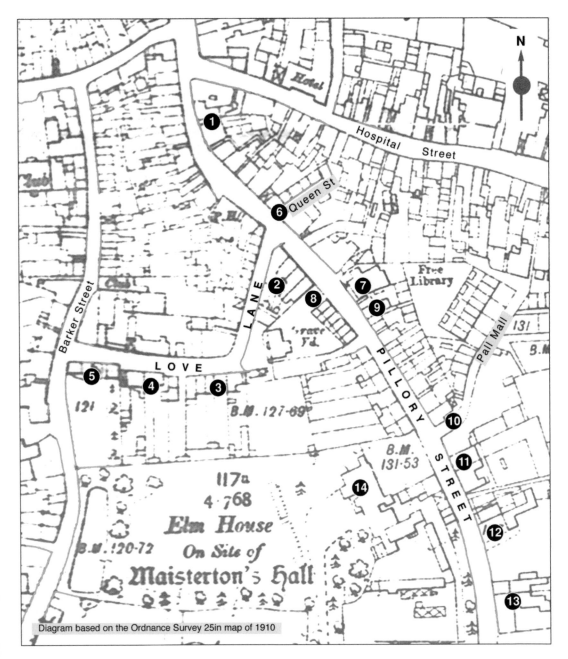

Diagram based on the Ordnance Survey 25in map of 1910

Pillory Street, Love Lane

1 3-7 Pillory Street
2 1-7 Love Lane
3 Meakin & Delves almshouses
4 23 Love Lane
5 25-29 Love Lane
6 Queen Street
7 The Old Gaol House

8 Fire engine house
9 29 Pillory Street
10 Pall Mall
11 55-65 Pillory Street
12 United Methodist Church
13 67-69 Pillory Street
14 Elm House

A painting by Herbert St. John Jones looking towards the square from Pillory Street, the George and Dragon public House is on the right. Beyond it is the Golden Lion and Chester's store on the corner of Hospital Street. Note how narrow the street was here.

A modern photograph showing the same view.

A photograph showing modern apartments in Love Lane, converted from the Meakin and Delves almshouseas.

Old black and white cottages in Love Lane. This area used to be called Mason's Yard.

were specifically for poor men, natives of Nantwich, over 50 years of age, belonging to the Church of England, and their wives.

In 1851, the following were in the almshouses:

Mary Hassall (widow of journeyman shoemaker)

William Basford (formerly shoemaker)

Sarah Butler (widow of shoemaker)

Mary Jackson (formerly shoebinder)

Elizabeth Butler (formerly shoebinder)

Joseph Tomkinson (journeyman bricklayer)

The last occupier of these almshouse in 1975 was Mrs Polly Davies, the widow of the last lamplighter in Nantwich. In 1977, the buildings were purchased by a developer and converted into a house and flats.

4. 23 Love Lane

In 1792, a smithy is listed here being in the occupation of Thomas Trevitt. In 1833 Joseph Trevitt was living here. In 1876, Thomas Walley was the blacksmith. Bell refers to Walley's shoeing forge here.

> 'In Love Lane, in the long ago, Walley's shoeing forge rang merrily, and if you stood awhile, or wandered within, the sparks, too, were seen to fly from every quarter of that modern and well-equipped forge. Of rotund appearance was the master smith, broad and stout, with a kindly face, and when a sharp frost made the roads treacherous, I have seen that forge full to overflowing with every class of horse, yet predominating, perhaps was the hunter, for Nantwich has ever been a notorious centre for several packs of hounds, within easy reach.'

The forge was eventually demolished in the early 1980s.

5. 25–29 Love Lane

Next to the smithy were three black and white cottages. No.25 Love Lane was a single black and white cottage. In 1896, Thomas Dooley, labourer lived here. It was still standing in 1953 but was demolished some time later. Nos.27 and 29 were two semi-detached black and white cottages. In 1896, John O'Hara lived at No.27 and Mrs Tomkinson at No.29.

6. Queen Street

Hall refers to the first workhouse or poorhouse in the town as being provided prior to 1748 by appropriating several houses in Queen Street for that purpose. This conflicts with his reference to a House of Correction in Beam Street which he said commenced in 1677, and in 1767 became the almshouses of Sir Edmund Crewe.

In 1788, Nonconformists inclined to Independency led by Henry Kitchen, a joiner and John Smith, a shoemaker, hired a room in the Queen Street paintshop of a sympathetic Quaker coachbuilder, Henry Welch. With a pulpit and two pews, it became a chapel. It continued to be a chapel there until 1801/2 when a new chapel was built in Church Lane.

The coach building premises can be clearly seen on the 1851 Town Map, consisting of a coach house, a wheel shop and a smithy. Only the chimney of the smithy still stands in what is now the Cocoa House Yard.

It is clear that later, conditions were bad in Queen Street as evidence from the Report into the Public Health Act of 1850 shows:

'Queen Street is an opening out of Pillory Street; it contains nine houses, but there was cholera in nearly every one of them. There are two privies, and one of them, used by four families, is entered by the same door as a house. Persons died in the houses adjoining it on each side. Mr Williamson said there had been much typhus in these houses for several years. The privy soil runs over the surface.'

In 1851, the following lived in Queen Street:

Joseph Whittingham (pauper, stocking weaver)
Thomas Wilkes (shoemaker)
James Peers (bricklayer's labourer)
Michael Digman (common labourer)
Joseph Owen (shoemaker)
Ann Astles (labourer's widow)
John Carroll (labourer)
Amos Weir (labourer)
Francis Carty (agricultural labourer)
Bell recalls an old lady who lived in Queen Street
'Who of my contemporaries, recalls living in a cottage in the Queen Street, between The Swan and the late Henry Welch's, a woman of great age, known as "Old Mary", who dispensed oranges, carrying a basket, and vending her wares at the Railway Station, an Irish lady I imagine.'

Since those earlier times, the cottages in Queen Street have been changed for the better and the buildings there are quite presentable.

7. The Old Gaol House

A low thatched house was for a long time the old town gaol. In 1788 it was reported as having two damp dungeons and two prisoners. The last Bailiff and Gaoler was James Topham who took office in 1825 and held it until 1862. In the 1841 census, James is listed as a glazier and as a plumber and glazier in 1851. In 1861 he is a market toll collector. His daughter Elizabeth lived there later on after her father died and Bell describes the little old cottage as being a model of neatness with its red flowerpot in the small curtained window. It was demolished in the early 1880s and a library built in its place. The building is now occupied by Nantwich Museum.

8. Fire Engine House

Hall refers to a fire engine house that was built in 1853 in Pillory Street, nearly opposite the gaol house, on land given by the Marquess of Cholmondeley. This did not last long as it was taken down in 1869 when the next fire engine house was built in Market Street.

9. Heath's Entry, 29 Pillory Street

There is a reference to Heath's Entry in 1860 where Thomas Heath, baker and flour dealer is listed as being at or in Heath's Entry. Quite possibly it would be on the corner. There were two cottages in the yard through the entry.

The Old Gaol House in Pillory Street. This was for a long time the town gaol. Note the hens in the street.

A pen and ink drawing of the same building by Ken Spibey.

10. Pall Mall

There is a reference to a school room in Pall Mall that was used as a temporary chapel around 1835 by the Wesleyan Methodist Association, but there is no indication where it was in Pall Mall. In 1869, Job Hilditch had a shoemaking factory here. In 1887, Francis Boston, boot and shoe manufacturer is listed at the Atlas Works, here. In 1896, it was George K Cooke, clothier and in 1913, Doody's clothing factory.

Victoria Buildings were a row of cottages built somewhere around 1870 (hence the name). This row was built at right angles and to the east of Grocott's Row on what is now Morrison's Car Park. Access to the properties was via a roadway from Pall Mall that went across the front of Grocott's Row. The terrace was still in existence in the 1970s but by 1977, only Nos.2, 6 and 7 remained. It is thought that these were also demolished soon afterwards.

11. 55–65 Pillory Street

At No.55 Pillory Street was The Railway Vaults. MacGregor refers to it as The London and North West Railway. Its licence ran continuously from 1861 to 1912:

> 'In 1912 this beerhouse, which was owned by the North Cheshire Brewery Co., was referred for closure under the Compensation Act of 1904. It was pointed out that the tavern had had eight tenants since 1886; that the sanitary arrangements were poor; and that of the six bedrooms that the house possessed, three on the second floor were unfurnished. It was also stated that the house was used "mostly by farm labourers". The house was forced to close the same year.'

A group of houses near Pillory Street end. When this photograph was taken they were being used as offices for Paxton's Plastics.

In 1913, John Harding, building contractor and timber merchant was living there, and in 1939, G N Dutton, electrician. It may well have been demolished some time after this as there are no further references in the local directories.

At No.57 Pillory Street in 1881 was a Temperance Hotel, the keeper of which was James Weir. By 1896, Mrs Sarah Hearnden had moved next door from the Railway Vaults and was the keeper of the Temperance Hotel. She was still there in 1913. By 1939, John Henry Harding was living there, and in 1953, G Dutton, electrician. There is no further reference to No.57 after this time.

At No.59 Pillory Street in 1881 was James W W Watts and by 1913 it had become the Temperance Hotel mentioned above. In 1939, 1953 and 1962, Walter Samuel Neal, antique dealer lived here. Some time shortly after this, it became offices for Paxton's Plastics.

At No.61 Pillory Street in 1881 was James Cawley Davenport, in 1913 Miss Hall and in 1939 Elizabeth and Harriet Hall. In 1953 and 1962 it was G Davenport. As stated above this then reverted to offices for Paxton's Plastics.

At No.63 Pillory Street in 1881 was William Chesworth, brick and tile manufacturer. In 1896 it was George Evans, clerk, then in 1913, George Evans, coal merchant. Thomas William Hall was here in 1939, George Woodward in 1953 and A Newberry in 1962.

At No.65 Pillory Street in 1896 was Henry Chesworth and Son, coal merchants. They were still here in 1913 and 1939. There is no record of anyone in this property after this date.

12. The United Methodist Church

The Pillory Street Chapel was built by the United Methodists in 1909 to replace the Ebenezer Chapel in Castle Street. There is a reference to this building in 1913 where the Minister is given as the Rev. J Longden. It closed in 1966 and was demolished in the early 1970s.

Pillory Street Chapel. It was built by the United Methodists in 1909 and closed in 1966.

13. 67,69 Pillory Street

At No.67 Pillory Street in 1881 was Elizabeth A Carven, milliner. Bell refers to this lady when writing about P H Chesters:

> 'Members of my family, in particular an aunt, the late Miss Elizabeth Carven, who carried on for a number of years a costumier's business in Pillory Street, was quite on intimate and friendly terms, and had a very high regard not only for "PH" as he was popularly called, but equally for Miss Chesters and all the family.'

In 1896, Edward Phillips, barman was living here and in 1913 it was Mrs Harriet Hobson. In 1939 it was William Brook, in 1953, Annie Brook. There is no record after this.

At 69 Pillory Street in 1881 and 1896, was Edward Bradshaw, tanner. In 1913, it was John Harding, timber merchant, in 1939, James Stanley Viggars and in 1953, John Treneman Smith. There is no record after this time.

The corner of Pillory Street and Station Road showing part of the Nantwich Motor Engineering Garage with the Pillory Street Chapel behind.

14. Elm House

The Pillory Street-End Mansion belonging to the Maisterson family was described as a very ancient house in 1622 according to Hall who is quoting directly from Webb's Vale Royal. However it is thought that the original Maisterson Hall occupied a moated site some short distance away on what is now a grassy area in Station View. In 1664, the Pillory Street Mansion owned by Thomas Maisterson had seven hearths, indicating quite a large house. Churche's Mansion is also listed as having seven hearths and so its size would be comparable.

The house was in continuous occupation by the Maisterson family until the death of Thomas Maisterson in 1768. It was then sold to Ralph Cappur, cheesefactor, whose son, George, took it down and built the brick building known as Elm House. The heads of the rainwater spouts confirmed the date of rebuilding with a date of 1797 and the initials GC (George Cappur). It was later sold to John Withinshaw around 1850. He is described as a currier and leather cutter and in 1861 employed three men and two apprentices. Ann Withinshaw is listed here in 1887. The de Trafford family are known to have owned the house around this time.

In 1896, Philip H Chesters lived here. In 1913, Samuel Sproston was the owner. He put it up for sale in 1935 and the sales particulars of Elm House of that date are of some interest. The house was described as a commodious town residence and one of the most valuable blocks of property in the town.

The front of Elm House shown across the lawn.

'Elm House, standing on the site of the historical Maisterson's Hall, substantially built of brick and slated, placed well back from Pillory Street, from which it is guarded by a pair of massive wrought-iron gates and pallisading, and a short circular drive.

The accommodation comprises:

ENTRANCE HALL, with ornamental Minton tiled floor
STUDY, communicating with a toilet room and WC
BOUDOIR, 18ft. by 16ft., with panelled dado
STAIRCASE HALL, with a conservatory and garden entrance
DRAWING ROOM, in Adam taste and a large French window overlooking the Pleasure Gardens 30ft. by 18ft, overall
HANDSOME DINING ROOM, 24ft. by 17ft.with large French window, fine inglenook fire hearth with ornate canopy
On the first floor, approached by an easy flight of Stairs and Spacious Landing, are 5 principal Bedrooms, Bathroom, WC Second Landing with Housemaid's Closet, Servant's Bathroom, WC, Linen Wardrobe, Sewing Room or Nursery.
On the Second Floor are 5 Bedrooms and a Store Room.
THE DOMESTIC OFFICES consist of Store Room, Kitchen with Triplex Grate, Scullery (hot and cold water laid on), Butler's Pantry fitted with cupboard and drawers, Butler's Room, Larder, Servant's Hall, Boot House, Footman's Room, Outside WC, Coal Store, and Chauffeur's Room.
In the Basement are 2 Vaulted Cellars, and an "International" One Pipe Heater Stove for the central heating to the main Hall.'

From 1939 to the mid 1950s when it was demolished, it was the residence and surgery of Frank Haighton the dentist.

Another view of the front of Elm House. The gentleman in the foreground may be the owner, Samuel Sproston.

8 HOSPITAL STREET

1. Chesters' Stores

In 1869, Philip Hale Chesters had his grocers shop here. Through the subsequent years, the business expanded and P H Chesters became known as a family grocer and provision merchant with premises in Pepper Street and High Street as well as the grocers stores on Hospital Street.

Willett recalls P H Chesters:

'But I must not omit the name of P H Chesters, whose grocery establishment at the corner of Hospital Street is still (1938) there. Like most of the business people of the town he lived on the premises and had about a dozen or so apprentices living in also. To get taken on by P H Chesters was considered a high privilege. They were called Philip Chesters' disciples when they marched two by two twice every Sunday to the Wesleyan Chapel, where they sat side by side in a long pew under the gallery.'

Chesters' store at the end of Hospital Street with the staff outside. Note the meat and poultry hanging up outside.

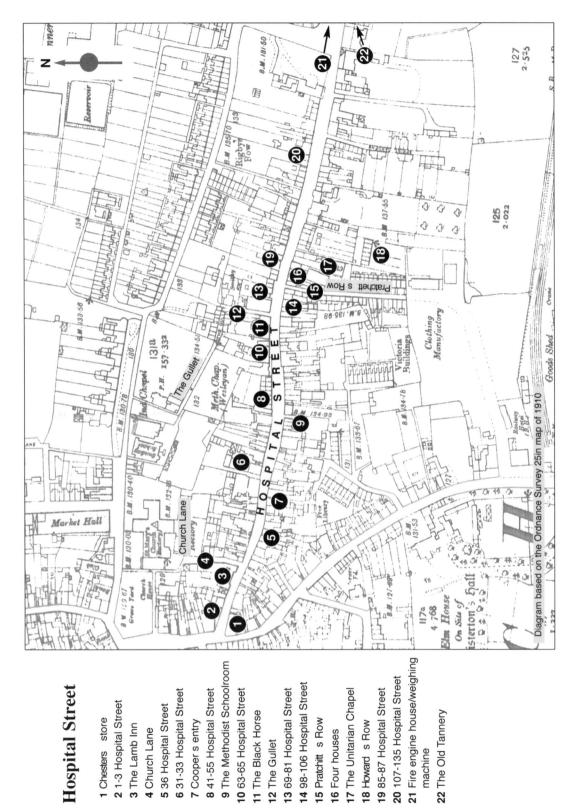

Hospital Street

1 Chesters store
2 1-3 Hospital Street
3 The Lamb Inn
4 Church Lane
5 36 Hospital Street
6 31-33 Hospital Street
7 Cooper's entry
8 41-55 Hospital Street
9 The Methodist Schoolroom
10 63-65 Hospital Street
11 The Black Horse
12 The Gullet
13 69-81 Hospital Street
14 98-106 Hospital Street
15 Pratchitt's Row
16 Four houses
17 The Unitarian Chapel
18 Howard's Row
19 85-87 Hospital Street
20 107-135 Hospital Street
21 Fire engine house/weighing
   machine
22 The Old Tannery

Diagram based on the Ordnance Survey 25in map of 1910

Bell also has this to say about the man:

'Philip Chesters was a generous man by nature. Many may be far better able to assess that generosity than I am, but I am convinced that to give in some way, whether a mere trifle, or a few coppers, a helping hand or a Christmas gift, whether a donation or a compliment, or a friendly or encouraging word appealed to the inner man, and gave him a real satisfaction. Yet he did not, by any means, I think, underestimate advertisement – it was instinct in him, and a great business asset.

He took a delight in being photographed with urchins and little ragamuffins on various occasions. Recorded, too, can be the fact that a down-and-out found in "PH" a helping hand, and a real friend of the Good Samaritan type. I have seen him in his shops at Christmas time shaking hands and chatting to his customers, wishing them with a smile that so well became "PH" the compliments of the season – and the poorest of his customers had the same hearty grip and the same expression of sincere goodwill, as did his more wealthy patrons. Nor was a suitable gift lacking for each as a memento of the yuletide season.'

Willett refers to a Nantwich Character propping up Chesters' corner:

'Jimmy Cash or "Cash Mash" as he was commonly called... spent a big portion of his days propping up Chesters' corner, prior to that great alteration placing a prohibited footpath in his way, and I imagine that for six days out of seven he, with others of a propping propensity, might be found there or thereabouts, an alternative parade ground was in the centre of the High Street and in front of the Union Vaults. Traffic was obliging enough to work round them or slow enough to give sufficient notice of an impending assault. The former was usual... I remarked that "Cash"! might be found in the vicinity of these rest posts, for six days out of seven, as an average or general thing, the seventh day being a Monday, coincided with the Crewe cattle sales, and "Cash" had a penchant for cattle driving. Walk to Crewe or from Crewe on a Monday, and some part of that four and a half miles you were sure to meet among the stream of traffic and herds of cattle "Cash," heated, dishevelled, excited and overworked. It was quite evident "Cash" took his cattle driving duties seriously judging by a redder than usual – redder than sunset – face and an agitated manner, accompanied by much grimace, ejaculation, gesticulation, stick brandishing and perspiration – running past himself and back again, attempting in vain to pass and surpass, take and overtake, his more active and four-footed charges. Always the cattle under "Cash's" charge appeared to prefer any road, and all roads to the straight and narrow one "Cash" had decided to firmly traverse, every passage, every open gate appealed more than that road, upon which Mr Jimmy Cash had decided to firmly tread. Yes, Cash was a character.'

It is well known that the building that was Chesters' Stores was pulled down, together with the two public houses previously mentioned at the end of Pillory Street, around 1910. Bell has this to say about it and its replacement:

'At the junction of Hospital Street, Pillory Street and the High Street, prior to the great alteration, many accidents occurred, the first two thoroughfares being very narrow, and what is known as "blind corners." Three points of interest gave much discussion and surprise at the time. First that after the improvement was made and the street widened by the rounding off of the corner, that there was any "Chesters" left to rebuild upon. The second was the general amazement at the splendid type and character of architectural building Messrs Chesters decided upon as their new "Stores"; it was likened by some, with its roof port-hole windows to the great Lusitania, which vessel had shortly before been launched. Nantwich had indeed, woke up. Thirdly, how a building could possibly be erected on such a wedge-shaped piece of land left after Garnetts (opposite) had been demolished. All, I think agree that the utmost that could be done was accomplished, and, what a bright change, from the low, dingy old shop that our ancestors had known as "Dicky Garnetts" with its blue and red apothecary's signs.'

2. 1,3 Hospital Street

Mention has already just been made of Garnett's shop at No.1 Hospital Street but going further back in time, it is thought that the old building may have been a public house. It may have been the Black Lion in 1646 as there is a reference in Hall to a fire that burned the Swan stable, the Black Lion stable and part of the Lamb stable, being all near together. The Swan was on the end of High Street where HSBC bank is now and it makes sense for the Black Lion as well, as being in a prime position for a public house, to be next door. It could well have changed its name to the Bear's Paw, whose licence ran from 1765 to 1791. The 1781 Town Rate Book lists Widow Newton as living here and MacGregor has Ann Newton as licensee of the Bear's Paw from 1779 to 1783.

What is more certain is that it was called the Old Barn and plays were held here before the playhouse was built in Dog Lane. In 1833 it belonged to Admiral Tollemache and the occupier was Samuel Garnett. An interesting advertisement dated 12 July 1823, reads as follows:

'S.GARNETT,
CHEMIST, DRUGGIST, etc.
Most respectfully begs to inform the inhabitants of NANTWICH and its VICINITY, that he has opened the Shop in the HOSPITAL STREET, lately occupied by Mr Pass, Cooper, with a general assortment of Drugs of the best qualities, and a *complete assortment of Groceries.* He hopes by strict attention to all orders he may be favoured with, to merit a share of their Patronage and Support.

S.G. Pledges himself to the Public, that he will send out no Drugs but what are of the finest quality, and free from all adulteration.'

Note that he is selling groceries as well as being a chemist, a rather strange combination. The building of wood and thatch was pulled down in or around April 1883 according to Hall.

In1896, Mr Maurice, dentist was here and in 1913, Mrs E R Pooley, ladies' and children's outfitter. At 1A Hospital Street was Edwin John Broomhall, butcher and above were Mrs M E Howell, art mistress and Herbert St John Jones, animal painter. There are several paintings of his that show what the centre of Nantwich was like over a hundred years ago. He was still using the upstairs studio in 1939.

The two old buildings next door between the previous building and the Lamb were demolished at the same time as the Old Barn in 1883. At No.3 Hospital Street in 1887 was Frances Plant, confectioner. There is no other reference to No.3 after that date.

A painting by Herbert St.John Jones of Garnett's shop at the end of Hospital Street. The artist had an upper room in the replacement building, as a studio.

A photograph of the previous view.

Looking towards the square. The black and white building on the right
is the left-hand side of Mrs Pooley's clothing shop.

Mrs. Pooley outside her clothing shop at the end of Hospital Street.
Note the nameboard Ye Olde Namptwyche Buildings.

3. The Lamb Inn

The earliest reference to the Lamb is given in *Saxon to Puritan* by Eric Garton. In 1554, William Chatterton, of the Lamb Mansion, groom-in-ordinary to Queen Mary, wife of King Edward VI, was granted a licence to 'keep a tavern in his mansion house in Nantwich Malbank Co. Chester, and to sell there wines by retail as freely as he might have done before the Act of & Edward VI and grant that no person shall retail wines in the said town.'

It is known that the Lamb was the headquarters of the Parliamentarian side during the Civil War.

In 1664, the Lamb had eight hearths making it the second largest establishment in the town after the Crown. It later had some long-serving licensees. Thomas Copestick held the licence for 43 years from 1798 to 1841 and William Oates, for 53 years from 1857 to 1910. The licence ran continuously from 1693 to around the year 2002 when it closed

The Lamb was also a post office. The 1691 Town Rate Book lists Richard Horton at the Lamb together with his post office. It continued to be the post office until the 1850s when the post office had moved up the street. It was also the excise office for the town, which had earlier been at the Griffin Inn in High Street.

The Lamb was rebuilt in the 1870s and the present façade has been retained from that time although it is no longer a licensed premises. Willett remembers Henry Hopley from around this time:

'Mr and Mrs Oates, the model host and hostess, their charming daughters, Miss Boughey, the perfect manageress, with her maidenly curls, full of prunes and prisms, and last but not least, Henry Hopley the 'king of ostlers.' How well I remember his activities Saturday was a great day. Conveyances poured into the yard and overflowed into the street, and filled the Church Lane. The large waiting-room in the Lamb Hotel yard was filled to overflowing with the purchases of the farmers' wives, and it was always a source of wonder to me how the porter managed to hand over everything committed to his charge, and how HH and his men had the conveyances in their charge ready and waiting at the appointed time; but it was done and without confusion. The hearse and mourning coach for funerals, the "turnouts" for weddings, all ready when wanted. Even the Fire Brigade was catered for! It was a standing arrangement for two horses to be always kept ready for emergencies, for as soon as the fire bell rang out the warning special harness was dropped on their backs by willing helpers, and often the horses were waiting at the Engine House before the firemen arrived.'

The old Lamb Hotel before the present frontage of 1860. This has now been converted into 2 restaurants and apartments with the front retained.

In a Civic Society Newsletter, John Craven quotes his mother-in-law's reminiscences of the Lamb:

'In 1906 the Lamb Inn was considered a very fine Hotel, the meat spit roasted and pastries made in a special still room. Mine host Mr Oates looked like a child's impression of an "Earl", always had a bread roll soaked in the spit juice with bacon for breakfast and attended Church every Sunday morning in a grey topper. The barmaid "Old Bough" had two large ringlets hanging down each side, (hair style of the day) ran the bar in a very orderly way and was well known to the extent that a Gentleman Frank Arnold taken prisoner in the first war was asked by the German Officer interrogating if he knew the lady with the ringlets at the Lamb Hotel.'

4. Church Lane

The Town Rate Book of 1794 lists 14 houses in Church Lane, not including the Rector's House. There were also seven stables, one for the Rector and three for the Lamb. Unfortunately it is difficult to identify individual properties from that list.

In 1801, two cottages were bought in Church Lane by the wife of Captain Jonathan Scott a non-conformist minister. These cottages were demolished and the Independent or Congregational Chapel built on the site. This chapel was used continuously by the Independents until 1842 when a larger Congregational Chapel was erected in Monk's Lane. The original chapel continued to be used as a Sunday School and as a venue for weekday services. In 1908, the chapel in Church Lane was sold and in 1913 it was probably used as a drill hall for the 7th Batallion, Cheshire Regiment. There is no further record relating to this building after this date.

At a Meeting in the Parish Church in 1737, it was agreed to erect a fire engine house at the back of the Lamb Inn, next to the Churchyard. This stood here until 1853, when it was taken down and a new engine house erected in Pillory Street.

In 1833, there was a shoe warehouse, currier's shop, college and leather house owned and occupied by Benjamin White.

The 1851 Census lists 15 households in Church Lane. The Heads of Household were:
John Ikin, corn and flour dealer
Frederick Tomkinson, blacksmith
Thomas Poyser, groom
John Walker, bellhanger and whitesmith (a whitesmith works with the non-ferrous metals e.g. tin, copper, zinc, lead and their alloys)
Isaac Egerton, pensioner
John Cooper, shoemaker
George Bowker, bricklayer's labourer
Robert Perrin, labourer
Thomas Hallmark, pauper (formerly carpenter)
William Smallwood, bricklayer's labourer and Chelsea Pensioner
Sarah Church, washerwoman
William Church, tailor
Mary Rigby, washerwoman
Eliza Carven, schoolmistress
Andrew Chater, Rector of Nantwich
Eliza Carven is remembered with great affection by her grandson Rupert Bell:

'I was accompanied by my Grandmother, the late Eliza Carven, known to a wider circle than the town's boundaries, for, in the private school, of which for so many years she was the Principal, I imagine with a justifiable pride she "educated" two if

"God rest you merry gentlemen.
Let nothing you dismay.
For Jesus Christ our Saviour.
Was born on Christmas Day"

A Christmas card of a drawing by Harry Johnson showing Jack Sutton, the last night watchman of Nantwich, outside cottages in Church Lane.

A painting by Harry Johnson of the same scene.

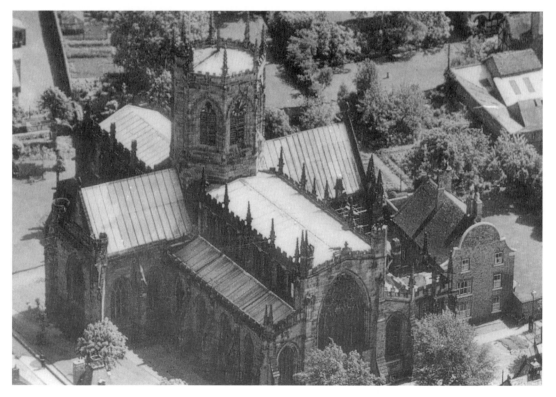

A postcard of Nantwich Parish Church showing the rectory with Dutch gable-end on the right.

Georgie Vaughan's house in Hospital Street. This is now the Hospital Street entrance to the Cocoa Yard.

Burgess's newsagents with Mrs Burgess outside. This is the same house as in the previous picture but at a later date.

Houses in Hospital Street. The white building on the corner of The Gullet is The Black Horse.

not three generations drawn from a wide area – long before the days of "free" education. She died in 1887 – on the last day of the year, and rests in the Friends Meeting House graveyard.'

She is listed in 1864 as being a schoolmistress in Churchyardside and from the position in the census i.e. next to the Rectory, the private school could have been on the site now occupied by the Parish Hall and Tourist Information Centre.

In 1896 and 1913, there are just five persons listed as well as the rectory. The previous rectory had been built for Dr Brooke around 1730, paid for largely by donations from the congregation. It had a characteristic Dutch gable end much in vogue at the time of building. It was pulled down in the early 1970s and the present rectory built further away from the church in the rectory garden.

5. 36 Hospital Street

In 1896,George Vaughan, bootmaker was living here in a black and white building. Bell remembers him:

'Georgie Vaughan... lived where now the Cocoa House have a new entrance. It was a black and white timbered house with tiny windows and a thatched roof. Vaughan, a thin, delicate looking man was of singularly quiet habits and retiring disposition; he would often, as I have seen him, repair the thatch in the breaking dawn.'

Some time later, it became Burgess' newsagents, and in 1913 it is listed as John Burgess, stationer and newsagent. By 1939 it had gone.

6. 31,33 Hospital Street

In 1792, this quite large building was a coach works and the occupier was Timothy Alcock. In 1810, it was occupied by Charles Welch and he was still here in 1835. In 1851, Edward Welch was working here with 13 men and six apprentices. In 1869, it was William James Welch. Henry Shakeshaft appears to have taken over the coach building after this date and he as listed as being at No.31 Hospital Street in 1896 and 1913.

7. Cooper's Entry

Between 44 and 46 Hospital Street was an entry leading to several cottages in a yard. This may have been Albion Place listed as having eight cottages in 1913. In 1939, there are just three mentioned here, with nos. 3, 4 and 5 Cooper's Entry. Some time afterwards they were pulled down and the site is now occupied by Cocoa House Gardens.

8. 41–55 Hospital Street

In 1808, when the Wesleyan Chapel was built, two preachers' houses were built on each side of the chapel. These buildings were identical although of course being mirror images of each other. No.39 still stands and is an antique shop.

At No.41 Hospital Street in 1851 was Sylvanus Williams, Supervisor of Inland Revenue and so it was no longer used by the Wesleyan minister. In 1896, Mrs Mary Ashworth lived here, in 1913 it was James Ormes, salesman, and in 1939, Albert Smith. The house was demolished along with the adjacent row of cottages c1970.

Nos. 43–55 consisted of a row of small cottages which were eventually demolished c 1970.

9. The Methodist Schoolroom

According to Hall, the Methodist Day and Sunday Schools were built here in 1840, and on Whit Sunday 1843, a fire occurred destroying a row of thatched cottages adjacent and damaging the Wesleyan schools. In 1869, James Hall was the headmaster. In 1876, it was William Thornicroft and in 1896 the head teacher was George Skelland with Miss Maskelyne taking the infants. This building was destroyed by fire in 1908 and the present building erected that same year. It also ceased to be a day school from that date.

10. 63, 65 Hospital Street

At No.63 lived William Morris, coal dealer and lath maker in 1896. Bell remembers him:

> 'Near the Gullet, too, was an old townsman named Morris, a coal dealer and lath maker, and I remember when the road was first macadamised, the coal daily delivered to Mr Morris was dumped down in the front of his house, as it had always been; the Council of that day probably on account of the dust created, rather than any damage to the road surface, decided it must stop, but Morris got over the difficulty by placing on the roadway, large sheets of stout iron, which while it may have preserved the road, neither lessened the dust raised, nor reduced the volume of noise created.'

There was a cottage behind No.63 and the entry leading to it was called Morris' Entry. In 1913, Miss Kelly, dressmaker lived at No.63, and in 1939 it was Mary Hilditch, dressmaker. Some time after this, the building was demolished along with its immediate neighbours to the East.

At No.65 in 1896 was Henry Crane, labourer and in 1913, Mrs Pinder, dressmaker, and in 1939, William Frederick Hassall, and Walter Slater in Morris' Entry. These buildings were demolished with the adjacent property some time later.

11. The Black Horse

At No.67 Hospital Street on the corner of the Gullet stood The Black Horse. Its licence ran continuously from 1844 until it closed in 1910. According to MacGregor, it was referred for closure in 1909 under the Compensation Act:

> 'The report gave a number reasons for extinguishing its licence. Very little trade was being done. The rooms had low ceilings; and the building generally was unfit for licensed premises. There had been eight licensees since 1897. One licence was enough for Hospital Street. In its favour it was admitted that the house was well conducted, and was used by "a respectable class of people"; and the house remained open. However, the inn was referred again the following year, after Hardy Fletcher had been made temporary manager in November 1909. The new report added that the *Black Horse* provided the worst accommodation in the vicinity, and that Evan Hayes had confessed to using the "long pull".'

In 1913, E Owen, hairdresser, was living here. Some time later, the building was pulled down and Rogers' Masonry Yard now occupies the same site:

Old cottages in Hospital Street looking towards the town centre.
The Black Horse can be seen on the left.

A painting by Archie MacKinnon of the black and white cottages shown in picture above.

12. The Gullet

In 1851, there were seven houses in the Gullet. The Heads of Household were:

Thomas Hough, wheelwright
William Hipkiss, cotton spinner
Edward Oatley, ostler
Joseph Chalk, conveyancing clerk
Charles Welch, retired coach builder
Joseph Clew, shoemaker
James Dutton. shoemaker

The list started from the eastern side of the Gullet and ended at the wWestern end i.e. the next building was the Black Horse. It is unfortunately difficult to identify these individual properties and the next list of occupiers in the Gullet does not appear until 1939. These were:

No.2   James Alfred Harvey
No.3   Jack Sandland
No.4   Doris Samways
No.5   Thomas Alfred Weaver
No.7   John Hopkins
No.9   Hezekiah Ruscoe
No.17   Ann Shakeshaft

The last house is included for reference only as it still stands and is still in the same family. In 1953, No.2 was no longer listed and Ronald Carr had moved into No.3, all the other occupiers were the same. These other houses were demolished some time after this.

13. 69–81 Hospital Street

A row of thatched cottages, some of them black and white, stood between the Gullet and No.83 Hospital Street. There is a well-known painting by Archie Mackinnon that shows this row of cottages. The end black and white cottage was the sweet shop of Mrs Rothwell according to Bell. It was demolished near the end of the 1800s and a large building erected on the corner of the Gullet, which still stands and is now known as Globe House. The other cottages were still standing in 1913 but by 1939, they had gone. Bell remembers them being pulled down and the great clouds of dust that the demolition produced.

14. 98–106 Hospital Street

At No.98, in 1896 and 1913, was Mrs Ellen Bouch, dressmaker. In 1939 and 1953, Harriet Alice Harding was living here. Some time before 1969 the house was demolished.

At No.100, in 1896 and 1913, was Charles Hampson, cabinet maker. In 1939, Jack Hampson, undertaker lived here with Constance and May Hampson, dressmakers. In 1953 he was still there but there is no mention of the ladies. As at No.98, the building was demolished some time between 1953 and 1969.

At No.102, in 1896, was Nathan Hough, grocer, baker and confectioner. In 1913 it was E V Oakes, grocer and baker. In 1939 it was Edward Shannon, grocer and in 1953, F Boffey, baker and grocer. As at Nos. 98 and 100, the building was demolished some time later.

At No.104, in 1896, was John Thomas Latham, painter and in 1913, Henry Parkes. At

No.106, in 1896, was George Tilley, chimney sweep. Johnson remembers the house.

'Adjoining Pratchitt's Row on the front of a little house was a sign which ran 'Richard Tilley, Sweep lives here; sweeps chimneys clean and not too dear; if your chimney should take fire, he'll put it out at your desire.' In 1913, Fred. Shone lived here. As there is no reference to this and the adjoining property after this date, they must have been demolished some time later.

15. Pratchitt's Row

The first ten cottages in Pratchitt's Row were built on the west side of the street, some time before 1833. The owner is thought to have been Mrs Pratchitt and the tenants in 1833, were George Meakin, John Hesketh, Joseph Holner, Charles Ravenscroft, Samuel Kettle, Joseph Johnson, William Yeardley, Jessie Prince, Thomas Jervis, and Thomas Ashley. These cottages can be clearly seen on the 1851 Town Map.

In 1851, the Heads of Household were:

Joseph Penkethman, tanner
Thomas Howard, agricultural labourer
James Brereton, agricultural labourer
James Prickett, agricultural labourer
Mary Judson, charwoman
William Cooper, shoemaker
James Wilkinson, chairmaker
Jessie Prince, shoemaker
Thomas Huxley, tinplate worker
One house uninhabited.

There is no mention of Pratchitt's Row in the 1896 and 1913 Directories. In 1939, Nos. 2–36 and 1–23 are listed. They were still there in 1969, together with Haighton's clothing factory and the business premises technically in Station Road of Doody's clothing factory, Slack and Mickle's Garage and Nantwich Motor and Engineering Co., NWF Building Department and the Cheshire County Council District Surveyor's Office. By 1974, Nos. 21 and 23 Pratchitt's Row had gone as had also Nos. 2–18.

The old Crosville Garage on the corner of Prachitt's Row and Station Road. Doody's Clothing Factory can be seen in the background.

16. Four houses between Pratchitt's Row and Unitarian Chapel

The 1851 Town Map shows four houses here. The third one along is shown as The Cheshire Cheese. In 1792, this was an alehouse called The Blue Boar, it then became The Blue Cap and then finally The Cheshire Cheese. In 1851, the landlord was James Westmore. It closed around 1861. It is difficult to identify the other properties due to the buildings here being renumbered in the 1960s.

17. The Unitarian Chapel

The Presbyterian (Unitarian) Chapel was built in 1726. Raymond Richards in *Old Cheshire Churches* published in 1972, describes it thus:

> 'It is a small building, but of the traditional form. Its length runs east and west and the pulpit, formerly in the middle of the south side was long ago transferred to the north side. The side pews are mounted up in tiers, as in some Calvinist churches on the continent of Europe. The exterior gables have almost a Dutch effect. (The chapel, becoming dilapidated, was completely destroyed in 1970.)'

There is a painting of the interior of the chapel completed by George Hooper in 1942 and it shows the pulpit and two brass plaques on the wall, one commemorating Joseph Priestley, the discoverer of oxygen who was a minister and schoolmaster here and the other to Philip Barker who founded Willaston School, which is now Regent's Theological College.

The Unitarian Chapel. Joseph Priestley, the discoverer of Oxygen lived and preached here. Preistley Court is now built on this site.

A painting by George Hooper of the interior of the Unitarian Chapel showing the pulpit in the foreground.

18. Howard's Row

The 1851 Town Map shows a row of six cottages behind the block of buildings with The Cheshire Hounds in the middle. This row of cottages is the site of Squire Barrow's mansion which can be seen quite clearly on the 1794 Fenna Map of the Town. In 1835, James Howard owned this property and soon afterwards converted it into the six cottages.

In 1851, the Heads of Household were:

Joseph Bolland, coal dealer
George Cobbe, ironmonger
John Brown, tea dealer
Margaret Newnes, letter carrier
One house uninhabited
Harriet Edwards, bootbinder

In 1939, there were six houses listed under Bolland's Entry and these would be the same ones mentioned earlier. There is no mention of these cottages after this date.

19. 85,87 Hospital Street

The 1851 Town Map shows two properties fronting the street here. At No.85 in 1896 was Mrs Eliza Dodd and in 1913, Mrs McGowan, hide and skin merchant. At No.87 in 1896 was Mrs Slater and in 1913, was Mrs Young. By 1939 these had been replaced by the motor engineers behind and so the two houses had been demolished.

20. 107–135 Hospital Street

There was a continuous row of cottages here stretching from No.107 right up to the Rookery shown on the 1851 Town Map. Mrs Mary Ann Hammersley had a grocer's shop at No.119 in 1896 and 1913. Her husband was Thomas Hammersley, the photographer. By 1953, Nos.107 to 121 had been demolished, and in 1969 the rest of the properties had gone.

21. Fire Engine House and Public Weighing Machine

On the 1851 Town Map at the end of Hospital Street, opposite Churche's Mansion, is shown a Fire Engine House and Public Weighing Machine. Johnson makes reference to the Fire Engine House and Bell remembers the Weighing Machine:

'At the end of Hospital Street an old landmark was removed when the town's weighing machine was demolished, and I imagine much daylight would be let into certain windows a yard or so away, that had, during years been obstructed; in fact an entirely new view must have presented itself to those cottages who had for so long been relegated into a background.'

In 1864 Henry Brown is listed as being clerk to the Public Weighing Machine, Hospital Street.

22. The Tannery, Hospital Street End

The old tanyard is considered to be the site of John Crewe's tannery. Sir Ranulph Crewe, son of John Crewe, tanner, is thought to have lived at Hospital House in Hospital Street in the 16th century. A century later and William Jackson, also a tanner was living in the same house and was connected with this tannery. In the Wilbraham family papers there is a lease dated 1655 concerning Willliam Jackson:

> 'Lease for 3 lives, by Roger Wilbraham of Wiche Malbanke Esq. to William Jackson of the same, tanner... a messuage/tenement and garden thereto adjoining with appurts. called St Nicholas Hospitall in Wich Malbanke, now in the holding of the said William Jackson;... the lessee covenants at his own cost to erect a sufficient tanhouse on some part of the premises, to sink the necessary pits and to make 2 sufficient gates for the way leading to the said hospithall croft for the said Roger Wilbraham.'

This extract suggests that William Jackson lived at Hospital House but that his tanyard may have been some distance away as the reference is to 'some part of the premises.' This could therefore fit in with the position of the old tanyard.

The 1691 Town Rate Book has a reference to a tannery at Hospital Street End with Thomas Pratchett being recorded as having a house and tan house on the site. The 1792 Town Rate Book lists Robert Taylor as the owner and occupier of the House, Tanyard and Stable. In 1833 it had become a Drying House, Tanyard and Stable owned by James Walthall Hammond Esq. (of Wistaston Hall) and occupied by J Barker. It appears to have closed some time soon after this date.

There were three cottages in the tanyard from before 1792. Later on there were six cottages there and these survived until at least 1910 after which they were demolished.

A photograph of the end of Hospital Street looking towards the town. The row of cottages on the right behind the Rookery have been demolished.

Section 2

NANTWICH OUTSKIRTS

9 THE BARONY AREA

BARONY AREA NORTH

1. Prefabs in Manor Road North

There was a row of prefabs erected some time around the early 1940S on the western side of Manor Road North. They may have been built earlier as there were 14 families listed here in 1939 but no numbers allocated to them. These later became Nos. 26 to 54 Manor Road North. There was also one on the other side of the road between Wallfields Road and what eventually became Davenport Avenue. These outlived their estimated life of approximately 15 years and were demolished in the mid 1970s.

A rear view of a prefab of the type seen in Nantwich. On the left is the kitchen, then the bathroom and then the two bedrooms.

Prefabs were erected in large numbers all over the country, particularly after the end of the Second World War, as temporary accommodation to ease the acute national housing shortage. In Crewe, some similar buildings are still being lived in.

2. Alvaston Farm

Alvaston Farm was situated just to the north of the Workhouse (which eventually became the Barony Hospital). It may well have provided food for the inmates there. In 1841, the owner was John Tollemache Esq. and the tenant was Henry Tomlinson. It was occupied by George Clayton in 1939 and stayed in the possession of that family until it was demolished in the 1980s to make way for the Barony Meadows housing development.

3. The Barony Hospital

It is thought that the only buildings demolished here were the wooden wards near the Middlewich Road. These were demolished in the 1990s to make way for light industrial development.

4. Vauxhall House

Nancy Dutton remembers a large white house at right angles to the Barony Road called Vauxhall House that was used to billet army personnel during the Second World War. It stood on the site of what is now No.82 Barony Road and must have been demolished soon after the war.

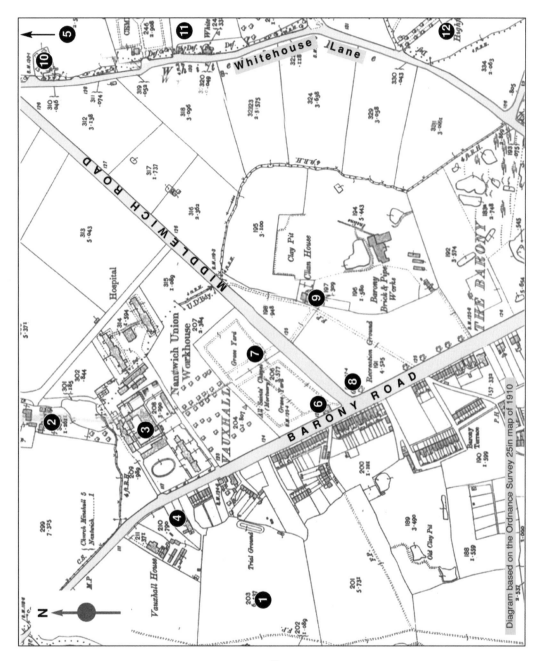

Barony area north

1 Prefabs in Manor Road North
2 Alvaston Farm
3 The Barony Hospital
4 Vauxhall House
5 Windy Arbour
6 Barony Lodge
7 All Saints chapel
8 Barony Gate toll house
9 Clan House
10 Sycamore Farm
11 Whitehouse Lane windmill
12 Highfield

Diagram based on the Ordnance Survey 25in map of 1910

5. Windy Arbour

According to Hall, Windy Arbour is a common name found on all the main lines of Roman roads, and signifies resting or sheltering places. As yet there is no firm evidence of a Roman road here, although one did pass within a quarter of a mile. Hall states that the estate consisted of an old mansion and demesne called Windy Arbour, which belonged to Richard Vernon, Gent. It was sold in 1788 by Charles Clowes Esq. to Messrs James, William and Thomas Foster, and it was still in the ownership of the family in the 1870s.

In 1841, the tenant was John Hockenhull. In 1861 and 1874, the tenant was Mrs Mary Hockenhull, in 1887 it was John Davenport, and 1913, Mr Cookson. A later occupier is thought to be Edward Birchall, and he is listed as being in Alvaston in 1939. Some time later on the house was demolished and there is now a scrap yard on the site.

6. Barony Lodge

When the cemetery at All Saints was established in 1849, a lodge was also provided for the cemetery keeper. In 1881 Thomas Prince was the occupier. In 1913 Leonard Wilkinson was the cemetery caretaker. The duties also included grave digging. Later on the caretaker was Herbert Boffey and he is listed as the sexton of All Saints in 1939. It is thought that the building was demolished some time in the late 1950s.

7. All Saints Chapel

All Saints Chapel stood in All Saints cemetery and was opened in 1884. It was hoped that it would attract residents from the local areas of the Barony and Vauxhall. Services were taken there most Sundays by one of the curates from St. Mary's Parish Church. In 1896 there was a service every Sunday Evening at 7 pm. In 1939 services were held on the third Sunday of each month with Holy Communion at 8am and Evensong at 6.30 pm. The building was demolished in the mid 1980s.

8. Barony Gate Toll House

There was a toll house on the corner of Middlewich Road and the Barony for the collection of road tolls by the Nantwich to Middlewich Turnpike Trust. Like most of the other toll houses it jutted out into the road. It can be seen on the 1875 OS 1st Edition map of the town. In 1871 the Toll Collector was John Scott and his wife Mary is described as Toll Collector's wife. The Toll House was demolished along with other toll houses around the town c1875.

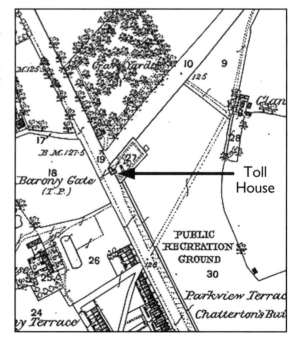

Barney Gate Toll House, Middlewich Road.

An aerial photograph of The Barony Hospital showing the wooden wards. In the top right-hand corner can be seen Alvaston farm.

The Caretaker's Lodge at All Saints Cemetery on the corner of the Barony and Middlewich Road.

9. Clan House

The 1792 Town Rate Books list the Clan House (although not by name) as Mr Yoxall's House, Garden and Stable, in the occupation of John Dimeloe. In 1833, the occupier was Samuel Sumner. In 1839 and 1847 the owner was Roger Young and the tenant was Ann Hollowood. Hall describes it as an old house, still standing on Beam Heath. In 1881 Ann Hollowood, farmer of 24 acres, is listed as living at Clan Cottage and this would clearly be the same building. Hall describes it as 'An old house still standing on Beam Heath.' It was the home of Hugh Broomhall, milkman. He died in the late 1920s.

Clan House is clearly marked on the 1938 OS Town Map and just to the south east is the Barony Brick and Pipe Works. The buildings were demolished in the late 1940s.

10. Sycamore Farm

The earliest reference to Sycamore Farm can be found on the 1875 OS Ist. Edition Map. It was later owned by Herbert Boffey, All Saints' Caretaker and tenanted by Mr and Mrs Capper. Reg Baker remembers their two daughters, Mary and Doris. Herbert Boffey is listed as living here in 1971 and 1974 and in 1977, it was E.Boffey. It was demolished after 1977 to make way for the new houses in Sycamore Close.

11. Whitehouse Lane Windmill

There is a single reference to the existence of a windmill in Whitehouse Lane. The Nantwich–Willaston Tithe Map of 1839 describes the large field immediately behind the White House as Windmill Field. This was in the possession and ownership of James Broadhurst who lived at Heathside Farm (now Willow Farm).This indicates that a windmill stood here at one time. Due to its close proximity, could the White House have been the miller's house?

12. Highfield

The 1881 census shows that George Ray, aged 55, Nantwich Postmaster was living here. The local directories in 1887 and 1890 show George Ray, farmer, living there so he must have retired from the Post Office and Highfield had become a farm. The farm can be clearly seen with a sand pit behind on the 1938 OS map.

The sand was used as a building material in the early part of the 20th century for new local projects such as the Council School in Manor Road, The Old Wyche Theatre (which became the Regal Cinema) in Market Street, and new buildings at Reaseheath School of Agriculture.

The farm came into the possession of the Massey family and then later it belonged to Harry Kingston who had a butcher's shop close to the Boot and Shoe in Hospital Street. It became an extensive poultry farm and was demolished in the early 1960s to make way for a housing estate and primary school.

BARONY AREA SOUTH

1. Wood Memorial Chapel

In 1881, the Primitive Methodists built a chapel on the Barony called the Wood Memorial Chapel. In 1896 services were held at 2.30 and 6 pm every Sunday.

In 1939 the minister was Rev. AGA Lees. Sunday services were at 10.45 am and 6 pm with the Sunday School meeting at 10am and 2 pm. The Guild met every Thursday evening, the Barony Methodist Sick Club every Monday evening and there was a Young People's Pleasant Evening on a Tuesday. GeorgePrince was the caretaker here for many years. The chapel closed in 1965 and the building was partly demolished. The site is now occupied by a builder's merchant and behind this is a local roofing firm.

2. Harding's Baronia Clothing Factory

Harding's Clothing Factory commenced operations in 1872. It was owned by John Harding of New Brown Street, Manchester and was their second manufacturing site. In 1882 there were 600 people employed. In the September of that year, the company was on the verge of collapse with debts of over £10,000 but within a week new orders were made with guaranteed work for three months and so the Company was saved from liquidation.

Bell remembers working there for a year after leaving school. He also remembers the long wing extension of the factory being built. This was in 1880 and the workers from the

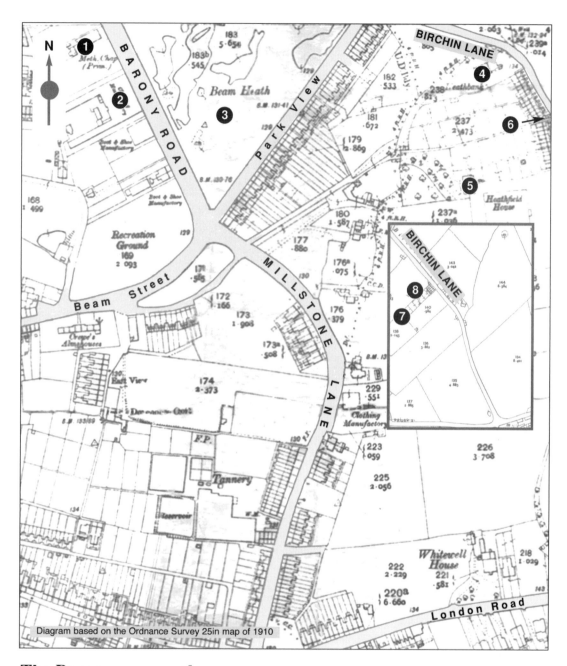

Diagram based on the Ordnance Survey 25in map of 1910

The Barony area south

1 Wood Memorial Chapel
2 Harding s Baronia clothing factory
3 Barony Park estate
4 Heathbank
5 Heathfield House
6 Birchin Farm

7 Birchin House
8 45-51 Birchin Lane

A photograph showing what could be one of Nantwich's Doctors. Behind him is the Baronia Clothing Factory and the Barony Primitive Methodist Chapel.

Manchester factory were brought to Nantwich to see the new building. They walked from the station to the factory behind the town band, had lunch, listened to the speeches, watched a cricket match and finally finished the day with a dance on the factory floor.

In 1897, it was registered as a limited company, but in 1903 the Hardings lost control of the business to a managing director they had brought in from Yorkshire.

In 1945, over 700 employees were working for the firm. The Baxter family ran the company until 1987 when they sold it to Kindler's Ltd who kept it going for two more years. Finally it was sold to property developers in 1989 bringing to an end 117 years of clothing manufacture on that site. The buildings were demolished in 1993 and a housing development of flats named Baronia Place was built on the same site.

3. Barony Park Estate

Temporary accommodation in the form of prefabs was erected on the Barony Park alongside Park View in the early 1940s. There was a total of 30 buildings here but they did not survive as long as the prefabs in Manor Road North as they were gone by 1959.

4. Heathbank

This was a private house near Heathbank Cottages but whose access was from Millstone Lane originally and then later on from Birchin Lane. In 1860 Samuel Harlock, Draper etc. is listed as living here. The 1881 census shows Josiah Gilbert aged 47, shoe manufacturer (of Gilbert's Shoe Factory) living there.

Before Dr Hugh Blacklay came to live here in the late 1950s, it was occupied by Mr Griffiths, solicitor. It was demolished in the early 1970s. Birch wood Drive estate now stands on this site.

5. Heathfield House

The 1881 census shows Thomas Pedley aged 29 living here, and he was still there in 1913. Nantwich Lawn Tennis Club had their tennis courts here for many years until the late 1970s when they moved to new premises at Alvaston. George Frederick Claypole is listed here in 1939 and it was later occupied by Reg Worthington who had a baker's shop in Park View. He is listed as living here in 1969 and 1974. The house was demolished at the end of the 1970s and Penlington Court now occupies this site.

A photograph showing the rear of Heathfield House. The pavilion and grass court of Nantwich Tennis Club can be seen. Penlington Court is now built on this site.

6. Birchin Farm

The distinctive brickwork pattern on a picture of Birchin Farm indicates that it was built around 1810. The two bow windows at the front are not original and were installed by Reg Baker's father. In 1839 the owner was Ralph Sneyd Esq. and the tenant was Peter Oakes.

In 1849 William Smith became the owner and the tenant was still Peter Oakes. When he died, the running of the farm was taken over by his widow, Margaret. In 1854, Phoebe Smith was the owner and Joseph and Thomas Bratherton were the occupiers.

In 1898 Mrs Elizabeth Prince sold the farm to Alice Baker in whose family it stayed until demolition in the early 1970s. Reg Baker remembers his father telling him about his surprise on returning home after the First World War. He had enlisted at the beginning of the war as Reg Potts, and during the time that he was away both his grandparents, Emma and Joseph Potts, died. As his parents had both died previously there was no member of the family to take over the farm. At the time Reg Potts was listed as missing in action. The family solicitors meanwhile let the farm to tenants without Reg's knowledge so that when he returned home, he found the farm in some one else's occupation.

Birchin Farm in Birchin Lane. This was built around 1810 and the bay windows added later.

Birchin House. This was built in the 1920s for Rupert Harvey from Harvey's Tannery in Millstone Lane. It stood not far from the end of what is now Harvey Avenue.

7. Birchin House

Birchin House was a large attractive private house built in the 1920s by Rupert Harvey from the Harvey family who owned the tannery in Millstone Lane. The house stood some way away from Birchin Lane, not far from the end of what is now Harvey Avenue and its front faced Birchin Lane. Reg Baker remembers gardening for Rupert who apparently always insisted in being addressed as 'Sir' in the correct manner of the day.

The house was sold to Mrs Boddington (of the Boddington's brewery family) around 1955, in whose occupation it remained until demolition in 1973. The houses in Harvey Avenue now occupy the land that previously surrounded the house.

8. 45–51 Birchin Lane

Four cottages, existing as two pairs of semi-detached properties were built in Birchin Lane just to the south of what is now Harvey Avenue, some time before 1875. It is not known who lived in them around that time but we do know that from 1955 onwards Mr and Mrs John Henry Mottershead lived at No.45 Birchin Lane. At No.47 from 1939 onwards was Mr and Mrs Thomas Boote. At No.49 from 1955 onwards was Albert Edward Boote. At No.51 from 1939 onwards was Lawrence P Wainwright. All four cottages were demolished in 1970 just before Harvey Avenue was built.

10 Millstone Lane, Crewe Road, London Road

1. Brick and Tile Works

The 1851 Town Map shows a brick and tile works covering an extensive area from Dovehouse Croft to Millstone Lane and there are three separate brick kilns shown. The land was owned by Plant Maddocks in 1792 and occupied by Messrs Nixon and Cappur. In 1850 Richard Barker is listed as a brick and tile maker at Beam Heath. Due to the proximity of the brick and tile works to the tannery owned by the Barker family it is thought that he may be the owner. That same year Thomas Barker died, leaving to his brothers Richard and Philip a piece or parcel of land called Dove House Croft together with the messuages, part of which occupied the brickyard. Richard Barker died in 1854. By 1875, the brick works had become gardens.

2. Dove House Croft

The 1851 Town Map shows a building named Dovehouse Croft in the south west corner of the above mentioned Brick and Tile Works. This site is roughly where East View and Scaife Road now meet, at the entrance to Maisterson Court.

The 1896 Directory lists four names in the Back Crofts, which are thought to be here, and these are:

Mrs Whittingham
Mrs Owen
George Fisher, labourer
Henry Owen, fitter.
In 1913 were:
George Grub, presser
Miss Sarah Ann Owen
Miss Martha Whittingham
Harry Owen, shoemaker

William Bailey, mechanic

This suggests that the building was divided into separate apartments. Reg Baker remembers the building existing as two separate cottages, Wallace Wainwright living in one of them.

3. Dewhurst's Clothing Factory

This factory was started in 1928 by the Dewhurst family who had several other clothing factories in the north west. There were just six factory workers to begin with. By 1968, its employees had grown to nearly 200 and it was still in the hands of the Dewhurst family. In 1998, it was employing around 120 staff and making sportswear for Adidas, but under the ownership of Lewing Ltd. It finally closed in September 2004 and a new housing estate will be built on the site.

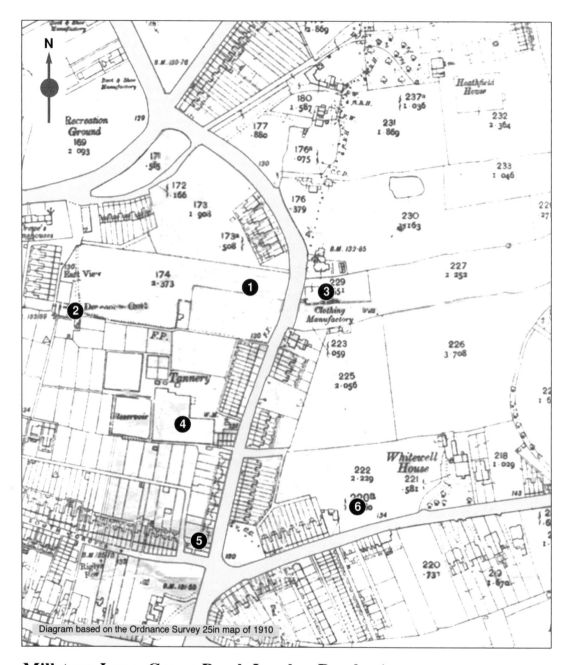

Diagram based on the Ordnance Survey 25in map of 1910

Millstone Lane, Crewe Road, London Road – 1

1 Brick and tile works
2 Dore House Croft
3 Dewhurst s clothing factory
4 Harvey s tannery
5 3 Millstone Lane
6 Heap s clothing factory

4. Harvey's Tannery, Millstone Lane

The 1851 Town Map shows the position of Harvey's Tannery, which is now the site of Monk's Orchard housing scheme. An engine house, bark house and tan pits are shown, with a large pool of water just to the west of the main tannery building. There were also three cottages shown within the tannery yard. At one time, the water supply was pumped from Cheney Brook at the back of Birchin Lane.

The tannery is thought to date back to the 18th century but the first recorded owners were Philip and John Barker who lived in Pepper Street in 1851. It may be that the J Barker, occupier of the tannery at Hospital Street end is the same John Barker and that the tannery closed in Hospital Street and opened soon afterwards in Millstone Lane under the same owner. In 1882 it was bought by the Harvey family in whose possession it remained until closure in 1972.

5. 3 Millstone Lane

The butcher's shop of James Ashley stood here at the end of the 19th century. A photograph taken of the shop around 1885 shows a cow outside the shop and meat hanging in the shop window. In 1896 he is listed as James Henry Ashley, grocer and butcher. In 1913 the shop was occupied by Fred Jackson, grocer, and in 1939 it had become Hollowood's General Stores.

In 1953, the provision shop was in the occupation of P King. From 1955 to 1966 S Cooper was here; in 1968 C Holbrick and 1970 W D Coram. Les Heath also had his shop here selling secondhand items for some time, after moving from Beam Street. The building was destroyed by fire in 1988 and has since been rebuilt.

3 Millstone Lane. This was James Ashley's butcher's shop in 1885 when the photo was taken. Note the meat hanging in the window.

6. Heap's Clothing Factory, Crewe Road

Heap's Clothing Factory actually began its life in Arnold Street around the 1890s. It moved to new premises in Crewe Road, south of Whitewell House in 1969. It later changed its name to Doody's Factory. It finally closed around 1995 with the loss of around 100 skilled workers. The group of buildings called Whitewell Close now stands on this site.

7. Taylor's Windmill, Crewe Road

There is surprisingly little information to be found regarding this windmill. It is clearly named on the 1777 map by Burdett. There are also three separate references in Hall:

Windmill Lane (now called Crewe Road) and the windmill that was blown down 'some years ago', this could have been in the 1860s;

In 1592, Richard Church bequeaths Wyndmill-field, and Malpas-field to his wife Margery, so the windmill must have been in existence then;

In the Church Registers 'Richard Steele, butcher, who was accidentally killed by a blow on the hinder part of his head from the sail of a windmill (near Mount Pleasant, in Windmill Lane, now called Crewe Road). Buried 18 January 1835. Aged 72.

In 1839, the owner of the mill was Sampson Cartwright who had the milling and bakery business at No.9 High Street that became Worsey's. Sampson Cartwright had also recently built Willaston Cottage on fields opposite Birchin Lane end. The miller who occupied the mill cottage then was John Lloyd and it is thought that he was the person who founded the bakery business of JJ Lloyd in Welsh Row. The 1851 census shows John Lloyd, aged 28, agricultural labourer living here with his wife Elizabeth.

8. The Mount

There is a reference to this house in Hall. It stood a little to the East of the windmill:

> 'One of the principal residences in Nantwich-Willaston, called "Mount Pleasant," was built shortly before 1828 by the late William Salmon, Esq. and is now (1883) occupied by his nephew, Henry Daniel Hill, Esq.'

In 1839, 1865 and 1874, it was in the ownership and occupation of Mrs Mary Meeke Salmon. The 1851 cenus shows Mary Meeke Salmon, aged 49, gentlewoman, living here. It was still in the ownership of Henry Hill in 1892 and 1914.

Reg Baker remembers that it stood empty for several years and during the Second World War, it was used to house evacuee children. The house is thought to have been demolished in the early 1950s and the present housing estate of the Mount built there soon afterwards. It is possible that the present Mount Drive road takes the same route as the original driveway to the house from Crewe Road.

9. Willaston Cottage

Sampson Cartwright built Willaston Cottage some time around the 1820s. It was known locally by the nickname 'Gingerbread Hall' as it was built on the proceeds of the thriving bakery business mentioned above. Sampson Cartwright lived here for a while after it was first built.

In 1865 John Mytton, agent to Lord Kilmorey, lived here and the 1881 census shows Samuel Garnett, chemist living here. In 1890 Mr Sampson Worsey is listed as living at Gingerbread Hall.

In1892 Sir Thomas Fletcher Boughey Bart. JP was here. Apparently he used Willaston Cottage as his base for attending hunts in the area. Over a period of forty years he was connected with the Albrighton Hunt, and for a considerable part of that time, he was Master of the Hounds.

In 1914 John Emberton JP was here and still here in 1939 but by this time he had been awarded an OBE. It was he who founded the local firm of cheese factors called Emberton Bros who had premises on the industrial estate in Weston Road Crewe.

In the 1960s it was occupied for about ten years by George Glover who had moved from The Elephant and Castle public house at Shavington. In 1973, it was in the possession of JAR Kavanaugh who later extended and converted the house into the Cedars Hotel. It became popular as a venue for wedding receptions. Around 1995 the Hotel was demolished and Cedar Grove now stands on this site.

Millstone Lane, Crewe Road, London Road – 2

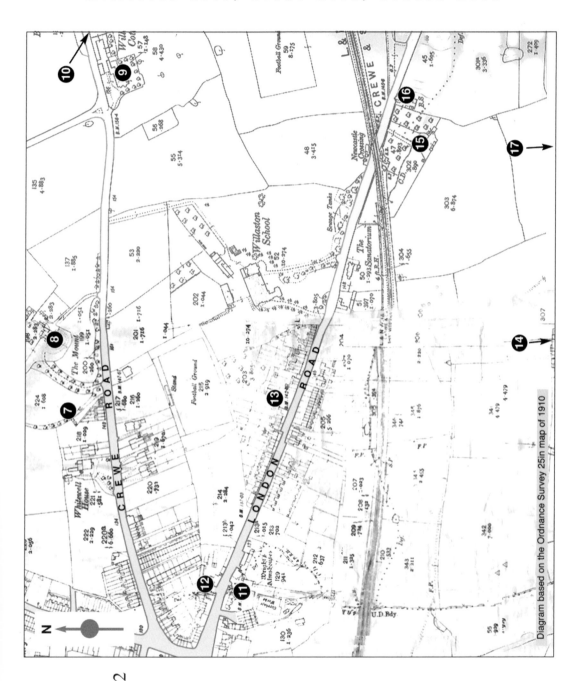

7 Taylor's windmill
8 The Mount
9 Willaston Cottage
10 Cheney Brook Gate
11 The Bull's Head
12 The Leopard
13 The Old Blot Hotel
14 Cronkinson Farm
15 Crossings Farm
16 Stapeley Toll Gate
17 Bytack House

Diagram based on the Ordnance Survey 25in map of 1910

A photograph of The Cedars Hotel taken in the 1990s shortly before demolition. The original building was called Willaston Cottage and built by Sampson Cartwright. It was nicknamed Gingerbread Hall after his successful bakery business in High Street. The building was later extended to become a Hotel. Cedar Grove now stands on this site.

10. Cheney Brook Gate

There was a tollhouse and gate for the Nantwich to Wheelock Turnpike Trust on the edge of Crewe road to the west of the still existing footpath to Stapeley. It was called Cheney Brook Gate in 1861. Like several other toll houses in the area, it jutted out into the road and it was designed so that oncoming vehicles could be seen from the front windows. The 1851 census shows James Holding, aged 54, agricultural labourer living here at the tollgate house with his wife Mary. It was demolished around 1875 along with other toll houses in the area.

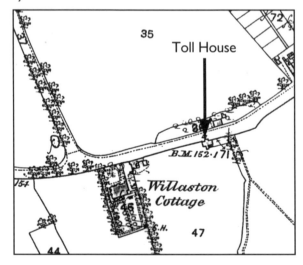

Cheney Brook Gate Toll House, Crewe Road.

11. The Bull's Head, London Road

A bull's head was the crest of Sir Edmund Wright who built the almshouses which stood adjacent to this property. This suggests the origin of its name. These almshouses were taken down and rebuilt on a new site in Beam Street alongside the other almshouses of Crewe and Hope. MacGregor suggests that this alehouse opened in 1767, just a few years after the inn, which is now The Leopard, across the road.

In 1845, the property belonged to Ralph Sneyd and there were 40 acres of farmland attached. Its licence ran continuously until it closed in 1983. There was a bowling green behind the premises.

The Bull's Head at the end of London Road with the original Leopard on the right.

12. The Leopard

The first recorded licence for this alehouse was in 1765 when it was known as The Horns. Its name changed to the Roebuck in 1789 and again changed to its present name in 1834.

The will of Richard Cooper of Saltersich, dated 1680, refers to a croft called Hart's Croft which he had leased from Sir William Bromley Knight. Although it is impossible to pinpoint its exact location, there could be a connection between Hart's Croft, The Horns and The Roebuck.

The most well-known licensee of The Leopard was Gomer Jones who was there from 1891 to 1928. The original Leopard had a building adjoining where Gomer produced his mineral waters. Simpson refers to it when writing about Nantwich Town Football Club:

'The Football Club NANTWICH TOWN had their ground at the rear of the Leopard Inn. It is still on the same site and approached by Jackson Avenue. This area was, in earlier years, an open field with a path from Inn to ground in the centre of it. Mr. Gomer Jones was the Innkeeper and proprietor of the Mineral Works alongside. A large entry divided the two buildings with a spacious room, above both entry and works. Here were the dressing rooms for both home and visiting players. A wood partition separating the teams at the rear. A door at each end was reached by an open stairway. So, spare a thought for the players of both teams as they ran the gauntlet of about 80 yards along the path before and after the game! The vociferous cheers, or at times jeers, that met them along the pathway was in itself a test of nerves. Boys and youths of course revelled in it and woe betide the visitors should they have the audacity to beat the home side!'

The old buildings were demolished some time around the 1920s and the present Leopard Hotel was built on the same site.

The Old Leopard showing Gomer Jones outside his front door.

The Wyche Anglers' Club. This was previously The Old Biot Hotel.
Wright Court now stands on this site.

13. The Old Biot Hotel

In 1887, Thomas Lovatt lived at a private house here at No.106 London Road. He was described as Deputy Superintendent Registrar to the Nantwich Union (i.e. The Workhouse). He was also described as book-keeper. He was still there in 1896 and the house was called 'The Hollies.' Some time later, the houses were renumbered in London Road and it became No.91. It was still a private house in 1939 and the owner was John Henry Philips.

In 1955 it had become The Old Biot Hotel and the proprietor was Ida Hines who remained there until 1964. From 1964 to 1966, the proprietor was Fritz Bailey. It became the headquarters of The Wyche Anglers in 1967 in whose possession it remained until around the year 2000 when it was demolished to make way for retirement housing called Wright Court with Wright Lodge being built close to London road.

14. Cronkinson Farm

The origins of the name Cronkinson are of some interest to the local historian. There is no doubt that the earlier name was Croncastle or Cronkcastle, suggesting the existence of a castle at one time. There is a reference in the Wilbraham family papers in 1586 to a pasture or croft adjoining a pasture called Croncastle. Later, in the will of Roger Cumberbach, tanner of Wich Malbank, dated 1678, there is reference to a lease of a field called Cronkcastle and the little meadow and the barn standing thereupon. In the inventory of the same year, there is mention of the same field and meadow called Cronke Castle.

The Tithe Map of Stapeley dated 1838 shows several fields variously called Corncastle, Big Corncastle, Little Corncastle and Long Corncastle and a track to the fields coming down from London Road, Stapeley to the North. The fields were owned by Thomas King Nickson and tenanted by George Bebbington. It is interesting to note that the names have changed through time.

Cronkinson Farm. This used to be called Cronkcastle Farm. Access was from Stapeley Terrace, across the railway line and through two fields. Harry Dobson lived here in the 1930s.

According to an article in the *Nantwich Chronicle* in the 1970s, the farm had been in the possession of the Dobson family for 200 years and was first farmed by Minnie Dobson's great grandfather. The 1838 Tithe Map describes the property as cottage and garden, owned by Thomas King Nickson and tenanted by Thomas Dobson. Minnie Dobson was born at the farm and lived for over 50 years and married Henry Edwards.

As well as being a working farm, there were two tennis courts and a pavilion where Nantwich Tennis Club met and league matches were played. Joe Dobson and Joseph Stonelake formed the Nantwich League.

The farm was accessed from London Road via Stapeley Terrace across the railway line and then along a track across the fields to the farmhouse.

Simpson refers to whippet racing on Dobson's fields:

'This is where the keenest of all racing took place and where the little teams of dogs from the North Staffs District were brought from to compete. Dobson's field was then, to be truthful, considered to be of somewhat ill repute not only because of the gambling but because of the fact that Pitch and Toss was played there, and that was illegal. According to my father's story look-outs were actually paid to keep watch at vantage points, or approach points! With only railway transport available in those days it is simple to understand how Cronkinson was popular with the Potters (so close to the station). Little activity in this sport has taken place since World War 1!'

The farmhouse and buildings were demolished in the early 1990s to make way for a new large housing estate. A new public house on this estate is now called Cronkinson's Farm

Crossings Farm.

15. Crossings Farm

The Stapeley Tithe Map of 1838 shows that Edward Kent owned the farm and the tenant was John Hassall. Well-known milk roundsman Bill Dobson had his dairy there. Firstly he delivered the milk with float and horse with a large milk tankard and various measures (half-pint, pint, quart etc.) on the back. Later the milk was delivered with a Jowett Bradford lorry, which apart from its normal duty was used for moving furniture from and to the Nantwich Market Saleroom and shifting bales of hay and straw for local smallholders.

Mr Fitton lived at Crossings Farm, which he purchased from Mrs A Dobson, and when he sold it to Mr Bebb, he went to live at the Old Biot Hotel as a permanent guest.

16. Stapeley Tollgate

A toll house stood on the roadside opposite the junction of London Road and Newcastle Road for the Nantwich to Woore Turnpike Trust. It stood on the same side of the road as Crossings Farm and jutted out into London Road, Stapeley. In 1861 Ann Brian, aged 31 is listed as the Toll Gate Keeper, and in 1881, Elizabeth Boote is listed as living at Stapeley Tollgate, after the road had ceased to be turnpiked.

It was still in existence in 1910 but was demolished some time after that. It is thought that the Pidduck family lived here for a while. The site was later occupied by a garage and accompanying bungalow but these were demolished in the 1990s to make way for the new housing estate.

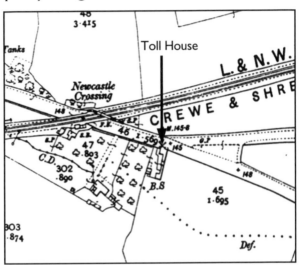

Stapeley Tollgate Toll House, London Road.

17. Bytact House

This house was situated near Cronkinson Farm. It was the home of George and Renee Woodcock who were well-known in the area for their involvement in local pantomime in the 1950s. Later on, Albert and Ada Knowles lived here. It is thought to have been demolished in the 1960s.

11 WELLINGTON ROAD, AUDLEM ROAD

1. Hillfield Place, Brick and Tile Works

The 1875 OS 1ˢᵗ Edition Map shows quite an extensive manufacturing site, thought to be a brick and tile works, in Hillfield Place. The only one listed in this area in 1874 was Henry Ray and Company, builders, brick and tile manufacturers and stone and marble masons, Broad Lane. In 1887 John Clarke, brick, tile and pipe manufacturer is listed at Hillfield Place. The 1910 OS 3rd Edition Map shows that this manufacturing site had now been built upon.

2. Parkfield

This large private house stood where Rookery Drive is now. In 1792 it was owned and occupied by Thomas Massie and described as House, Outbuildings, Gardens, Orchard etc. In 1833 it was occupied by Mrs Richardson. In 1845 the owner was Mary Massey and the occupier was John Richardson. It was known then as The Lodge.

In 1850 Thomas Lewis, draper lived here. In 1864 Edward Swinfen Bellyse MDEsq. was living here. By 1869 it had been renamed Parkfield and the occupier was Mrs Emily White. In 1874 and 1881 Levi Leigh was living here.

In 1885 Parkfield's most famous resident, Albert Neilson Hornby had come to live here from Church Minshull. He had bought a three-storey house standing in 28 acres called Parkfield. He lived here until he died in 1925. *The Cricketing Squire* by WE Hoole, written in 1991, gives a fascinating insight into this remarkable man and below are some snippets from the book:

In the most well-known poem on cricket called 'At Lords' by Francis Thompson, the first verse begins with these lines:

> 'It is little I repair to the matches of the Southron folk' and ends with 'O my Hornby and my Barlow long ago.'

This poem was written in 1907 and refers to a particular match that the writer had seen when he was eighteen in 1878. In this match, Lancashire CC were playing for the first time at Old Trafford against a formidable Gloucestershire side fielding Dr WG Grace and his two brothers. Although the match ended in a draw, Hornby and Barlow were the Lancashire heroes, with Hornby scoring a century out of a total of 150 in the second innings. For Gloucestershire, WG Grace scored 32 and 58 not out and also took 4 wickets. This match left Francis Thompson with an unforgettable memory that resulted in his writing the poem 29 years later.

Some four years after that match, in 1882, Albert Hornby captained the England side at the Oval against Australia in what is considered to have been the greatest Test Match ever, according to Sir Neville Cardus.

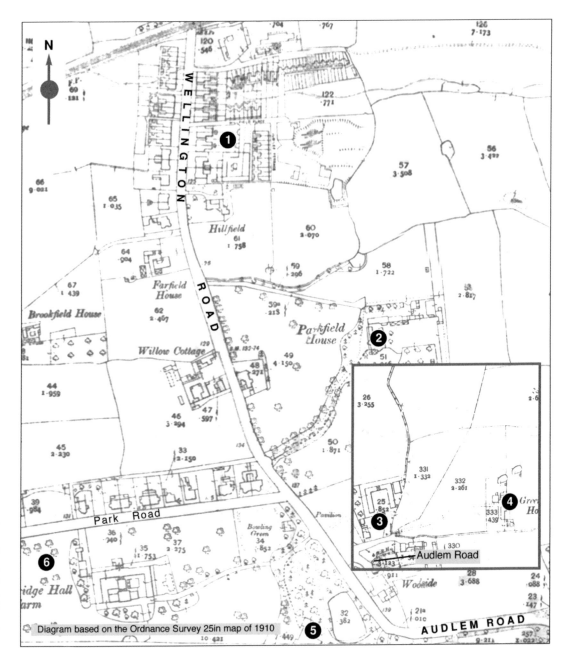

Diagram based on the Ordnance Survey 25in map of 1910

Wellington Road, Audlem Road

1 Hillfield Place brick and tile works
2 Parkfield
3 Wood View
4 Greenfield House
5 The Brine Baths Hotel
6 Brine House

Hornby considered his batting line-up so strong that he put himself in at No.10 in the first innings, he only scored 2 runs. He did however open the second innings with WG Grace but only scored 9 when bowled out with the score on 15. The next ball, Barlow was out for nought, the crowd went silent! WG made a respectable 33 but it was not enough to save the day and England lost by 7 runs.

This obituary was placed in the *Sporting Times* at the end of that week:

'In affectionate Remembrance of English Cricket which died at the Oval on 29th August 1882.
Deeply lamented by a large circle of Sorrowing Friends and Acquaintances.
RIP
NB The body will be cremated and the Ashes taken to Australia.'

The next year, a team under the captaincy of Ivo Bligh sailed to Australia to recover the Ashes. England won the series and the nebulous Ashes were given a more solid form when some Melbourne ladies burnt a bail used in the final game and gave the ashes to the England captain. The symbolic wooden urn stands permanently in the Imperial Cricket Memorial at Lords.

Hornby had a mania for stealing short runs, he certainly held the record for running men out. Arthur Shrewsbury, in a Nottsinghamshire match, on the early dismissal of Hornby, the Lancashire captain, remarked that he was sorry Mr Hornby was out. On being asked what he meant by being sorry one of the best Lancashire batsmen was out, he replied, 'Well if he had stayed in, all the rest would have been run out!'

Hornby took a delight in bringing the Lancashire team to play against Nantwich and district. On one occasion, the village band was in attendance and Kermode, the Lancashire bowler, while batting, hit a ball that burst the big drum.

When the hunting season was on, several of the cricketers received invitations to come to Parkfield and spend a few days following the hounds. Apparently they were most enjoyable outings and they were well entertained.

What of the man himself ? He was short of stature standing at only five foot three and because of his size was nicknamed 'Monkey' at Harrow and although it stuck with him all his life he never objected to its use.

He was a fine captain, possessed an iron constitution and was capable of a large amount of strenuous work. He was never heard to say that he was tired after a long day in the field and did not expect others to be either. He was a strict disciplinarian. He was also a true all-round sportsman, captaining the England rugby team and also played for Blackburn Rovers, scoring a goal for them in an FA Cup match.

He married wealthy Sarah Ingram whose father owned *The Illustrated London News*. He was a Justice of the Peace from 1896, Chairman of Nantwich Conservative Association and became the first County Councillor for Nantwich. He served in the Cheshire Militia and was one of the oldest members of the Beam Heath Trust in 1919. He died in 1925 aged 78. His grave with a cricketing headstone can be seen in Acton churchyard.

In a private publication *The Life and Times of a Great Victorian Sporting Hero AN Hornby* by Peter Wall, there is a description of life at home taken from the Athletic Journal in 1887:

'A sketch of the Lancashire Captain at home is easier ordered than written, Mr Editor, as Mr Hornby is not much at home in the summer months.
It was at Church Minshull where our hero first went to live after his father's death he went to Parkfield , where we intend to picture him at home. Mr Hornby's mother, a comely dame, still lives in Welsh Row, Nantwich and his sister, Mrs Captain Massey resides at Poole Hall. The most popular man of the lot is Albert, our Lancashire Captain and without more ado, we will set to work and depict our champion as an

amiable husband and father of four of the sharpest, though small lads, it is possible to put in a row. Albert the eldest and just 11years old, has just gone to Elstree School at Harrow and there's Walter, George and John still at home ruled by a governess, when they are not climbing trees or setting a dog to have a bit of fun with the tame rabbits in the enclosure at the back of the house.

Parkfield is a grand old looking house, standing in the centre of some 17 acres and, in the front, cattle are grazing, in total ignorance of the grandeur of the house or the importance of their owner. The first introduction one gets after plodding up a long walk is the sight of a good specimen of boarhound and an old hunter, a relic of past greatness, is cantering in a nearby paddock. Here Mr Hornby has left the old thing to pass its last few days in peace and plenty and within a few yards of the stables, which when in the full swing of the hunting season, accommodate some 7 horses for Mr Hornby and 3 for Mrs Hornby, whilst there are a few cobs for the boys. The Farmyard, which includes a piggery, duckery and henery (sic) are fitted up in the latest fashion and a run through the stables is worth one's while.

On the other side of the house is the lawn-tennis court and the cricket ground which was opened at the beginning of this season and here Mr Hornby indulges in a little practice with 'Tad' as the Nantwich professional is called as a bowler and the lads field or at least Master Albert, the others like a bit of batting but fielding is not in their line yet.

The house inside is indicative of luxury but still home; the place is fitted up for comfort and if Alfred is wanted, there is no need to send a girl round to the harness room, there's a telephone to take the message and by the time the visitor has got his coat on, there's a conveyance to take him to the station.
Mr Hornby sets all things aside in the summer for cricket, though at home he occasionally takes a turn at lawn tennis. Billiards are too slow and the Billiard room at Parkfield has been turned into a nursery.'

In the same book by Wall there are details of a sale of the contents of Parkfield in 1928 on the death of Mrs Hornby. There were 1100 items in the sale and their number and variety reflected the quality of life which had been enjoyed at Parkfield.

The rooms are listed as follows:
Vestibule and Entrance Hall, Morning Room, Drawing Room, Dining Room, Sitting Room, Billiard Room, Maid's Pantry, Butler's Pantry, Kitchen, scullery, larder and cellar, & 7 Principal Bedrooms, and 3 Maid's Bedrooms and a Saddle Room.

The effects included:
Bay horse (good jumper)& aged pony, dog cart, brougham, 2 victorias, 2 shooting brakes, 3 horse caravans, 3 tons mangolds, straw, oats and hay, Ford touring car, good working order,3 poultry houses with runs and a 20 egg incubator, 2 dog kennels, bird cages, sheep troughs, scythes, mowers and rollers (man and pony power).

29 sets of silver items, ranging from carving dishes, Georgian salvers etc. 50 sets of plate and cutlery, 45 sets of glass and china, including engraved glasses and goblets, 9 oil paintings including a Morland.

Lots of furniture, including a pair of brass twin bedsteads and burr walnut items from Bedroom No.1

Many items reflecting the sporting interests (though not cricket or shooting) including fishing rods for salmon and trout, tennis nets and racquets, croquet sets, a billiard table (without a cloth!) balls and cues. In the evening, the Hornby family could relax listening to a player piano.

The eldest son AH Hornby inherited the Parkfield estate, but this was eventually sold to a property developer.

In 1939 Leslie Bradford Harvey was living at Parkfield. By 1953, it had been divided into two separate halves. In the eastern half lived Mr and Mrs Bert Skidmore from the chemist family and the other half was occupied by Robert Linton Millward. In 1958 Skidmores were still there but Frank Cotterell and family were in the other half. There were three Cotterell children, Anne, Frank and Jane. They were still there in 1962 but by 1966, the Cotterell family had gone leaving the Skidmores in residence. They must have left soon after as Parkfield was demolished around 1968.

In 1984, a cricket correspondent in the *Daily Telegraph* commented on the sad state of English cricket and headed his column 'O my Hornby'.

Parkfield, the home of A.N.Hornby showing the South facing wall with bay window.

Horse and carriage at the front door of Parkfield.

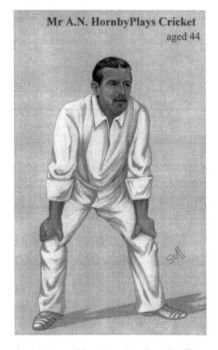

A painting titled Monkey by "Stuff".

A.N.Hornby standing on the left of two friends at the front door of Parkfield.

3. Wood View

The house was built fairly soon after 1875 as it is not shown on the OS First Edition Map of 1875 but in 1881 William Galley was the occcupier. There were quite extensive stables to the rear of the house covering three sides of a courtyard, with the two arms at each side of single storey and the main block of two storeys. There was later a flat above the stables. In the early 1950s Wood View and stables were owned by Mr Kenneth Mason.

Around 1957 it was sold to Samuel Hill who had trained racehorses in India, the stables being used for his horses. He continued living there until the buildings were demolished in the early 1990s when the new housing estate incorporating Cronkinson Farm was begun.

Wood View, Audlem Road. Samuel Hill, who had trained racehorses in India, lived here from 1970 to the 1990s.

Wood View stables exterior. There were two wings on each side, at right angles to the central block, one end of which can be seen on the left.

Greenfield House. Henry Martin, farmer lived here in 1939.

4. Greenfield House

There is very little known about Greenfield House. In 1939 Henry Martin, farmer, lived here. It is known that Samuel Hill owned both Wood View and Greenfield and is thought to have used the farm for his horses. The house and outbuildings were demolished in the mid-1990s for the new housing estate mentioned immediately above.

5. The Brine Baths Hotel

In the *Brine Baths Hotel, Nantwich* by Derek Hughes, there is much information regarding the history and demise of the hotel. It appears that Isaac Horton, a local currier or leather dealer bought land in the Audlem Road, Park Road and Shrewbridge Road area around 1790. This land included Shrewbridge Farm, which supplied vegetables and dairy produce to Nantwich Mill at the bottom of Mill Street. When Isaac Horton died in 1803, his estate was left to his daughter Mary and in 1805, she married Michael Bott, who had become the mill owner in 1795. Mary died in 1822 and left the estate to her husband Michael. In 1825 Michael Bott retired from active participation in the running of the mill and remarried in 1828. The following year, he had the old Shrewbridge Farm demolished and on its site he arranged to have built for his bride a handsome white stone mansion:

> 'A large part of the estate was laid out to parkland and gardens surrounding the mansion and a new farmhouse had also been built, now to be known as Shrewbridge Hall Farm. There was an imposing entrance and driveway off Broad Lane (now Audlem Road) and the road on the northern extremity of his estate was called Shrewbridge Park Road (now shortened to Park Road). Over the years Michael had bought more land and the total extent of his estate was now 108 acres extending as far as Coole Lane. These were the prosperous years for Michael Bott who was now a leading figure in the town and supporter of St Mary's Church. His second wife bore him four sons, John, Thomas, Charles and Philip. The only thing which probably displeased him was that his new mansion, which he had called Shrewbridge Hall,

was more commonly referred to as Bott's Hall!! After 18 years of marriage to his second wife, Michael died on 29th December 1846 and joined his first wife in Wybunbury churchyard.'

Wall summarises the later history of the estate.

Michael Bott's second wife died that same year and the estate was left in trust to his sons to be sold when the youngest had reached 21. The property was put out to lease.

In 1861, it was let to William Henry Hornby, father of A N Hornby, mentioned above at nearby Parkfield. In fact A N Hornby lived at Shrewbridge Hall until his marriage in 1876. In 1878, the estate was sold to J M Bennett, a cotton magnate. In 1880, it was converted into a sanatorium and a brine well sunk.

The hall was purchased in 1883 by the Nantwich Salt Springs Hotel Ltd, and greatly expanded. It was opened in1883 as The Brine Baths Hotel with facilities for permanent residents, with visitors undergoing hydro treatment. It also provided an ideal base for members of the hunting fraternity with suites reserved during the season and stabling for 50 horses.

Hughes describes the early days of the Hotel:

'A Tariff and souvenir guide describes the Hotel "as being delightfully situated in a fine park of one hundred and twenty acres comprising a fine entrance hall and corridor, spacious dining and drawing rooms, a library, billiards room, eight private sitting rooms, numerous bedrooms (single and double) and a well appointed suite of brine and medicinal baths. The Baths are actually within the Hotel, a convenience greatly appreciated by the large number of visitors who have already obtained relief by the treatment, the benefits are very great, especially in cold or wet weather. Well lighted, efficiently heated and well ventilated, scrupulous care is exercised in the promotion of ideally healthy conditions.

The grounds surrounding the Hotel have been laid out with great taste and skill, the gardens being particularly beautiful. Lawn tennis courts, a golf course, a bowling green, a well stocked conservatory, a pleasant terrace overlooking the lawn and several paths bordered with trees and shrubs are the principal attractions."

There were in fact 54 bedrooms in the Hotel. It was originally lit by gas but within very few years the Hotel had its own generator installed for electricity. This was situated close to Park Road and in its early years was rather noisy and subject to several complaints from the well-to-do residents of Park Road.'

The Guide goes on to describe the baths which were situated in a purpose built single-storeyed suite, reached by an entrance at the rear of the main corridor of the Hotel:

'... The brine was pumped from the Bathing Meadow (or Salt Ley Meadow as it was later known) by the means of pipes, with a diameter of about 4 inches, which were suspended on poles just above head height to the boiler room at the Hotel and then to the high reservoir. There were, in fact, 8 treatment baths in the suite.

... The area was extremely convenient for the wealthy classes who wished to follow up to 5 hunts which flourished. The South Cheshire Hounds hunted on Tuesdays and Fridays, the North Cheshire Pack on Mondays, Wednesdays, Thursdays and Saturdays. The Hotel was also in easy reach of the North Stafford, the North Shropshire and Sir Watkin William Wynn's Hunts. Several keen huntsmen used to rent one of the private sitting rooms or apartments on the ground floor for the Hunting Season, bringing their mounts with them to be stabled at the Hotel. They would sometimes be accompanied by their servants who would be accommodated in servants' quarters with the permanent Hotel staff. No doubt the mounting block

The Brine Baths Hotel. View of the front showing the original building.

The same frontage from a different angle.

The Brine Baths Hotel showing the conservatory and extension.

The Brine Baths Hotel in its grounds.

outside the main entrance was well used. It was, therefore, only natural that the Annual Hunt Ball was regularly held at the Hotel in the fine Ballroom adjacent to the Dining Room. Amongst the famous people staying at the Hotel in those late Victorian days were the Duke of Westminster who regularly took an apartment for the hunting season. On one occasion the Duke of Teck, father of Queen Mary, who was formerly Princess of Teck, also took an apartment for the season.

... Despite the open appearance of affluence, the Hotel lost money during these early years. In fact, it never made a great profit throughout its comparatively short existence. By the year 1902 the debts had mounted up and the Company went into liquidation on 26th of March... However a new Company was registered with an authorised capital of £20,000.

The Hotel survived these crises and kept up to date with all the modern developments. It was now lit by electricity and connected to the new telephone system. It was, in fact, one of the first premises to be connected to the new Nantwich Telephone Exchange with the telephone number Nantwich 10.

Mr Worsey (the Manager, who was named after his grandfather Sampson Cartwright, miller and baker who built Willaston Cotttage), filled the Hotel with many valuable works of art. In the entrance hall were several notable paintings, including 6 Morlands, and among the pieces of oak furniture was a French canopy chair, a unique Welsh dresser and a quaint fireside settle. In the long corridor were several valuable articles, including a 15th Century cabinet, some antique chairs, Jacobean, Chippendale and Italian marquetry and also a beautiful set of armchairs.

In the principal room were specimens of rare china (Sevres, Dresden and Crown Derby etc.) and a fine collection of Oriental bowls and vases. The chief specimens of Wedgwood china were a Portland vase and a beautiful plaque.

The drawing room was furnished in marquetry; the frescos illustrated Milton's *L'Allegro* and in the dining room was a unique frieze composed of two dinner services which was much admired by the guests at the Hotel.

In 1912 there was a widely reported burglary at the Hotel when many of the works of art, including one of the valuable paintings by the artist, Morland, were stolen.

... The Brine Baths Hotel was to some extent unique in that it was a mixture of several things. It was a Hydro, a centre for the Hunting fraternity of South Cheshire, a luxury Hotel and an old people's home. At the same time, it retained the atmosphere of a gentleman's country house.

... Before we leave the Hotel itself, I will make mention of the permanent guests who were resident between the wars. They were an assorted bunch. There was Rupert Harvey (later to build and live in Birchin House) who lived at the Hotel because he was a single man and found it more convenient than living at home or in an apartment of his own. There was Mrs Marshall, a wealthy lady who lived at the Hotel with her lady companion. Frank Hollowood, the chauffeur employed by the Hotel, used to take them on shopping trips into town or on runs into the South Cheshire countryside. He described Mrs Marshall as a charming lady. She often left him a parcel of fresh salmon on the back seat of his Daimler Landaulette.

There was also Mr and Mrs Pilling. Mr Pilling was a cotton broker from Manchester. He used to tell people that he and his wife lived at the Hotel as his wife had difficulty in "retaining domestic staff". They owned a Rolls Royce with a fabric covered body of leatherette which was all the vogue in the thirties. They employed a chauffeur called Mr Watson who lived in Wellington Road nearby.

Then there was a lady called Mrs Hallmark who was a close friend of Mr Worsey and worked at Worsey's Confectioners shop in the town.

Next there was Mrs Knight, a lady of about 70 years, who lived in her room with a verandah on the first floor. She was an amateur artist who also took a great interest in wild birds, which she used to encourage onto her verandah by feeding them with "Kunzle" cakes which she had taken from the Conservatory after afternoon tea. It was very rare that there were no birds to be seen on her verandah!

Major Ashton and his wife were well known to the staff. He was a retired Army Officer who was always smartly dressed in thornproof tweeds and had a military bearing. He always wore brogue shoes. He had an interest in gardening and often passed the time of day with the outdoor staff. His wife used to ride to the Hunt. On one occasion a member of staff recalled that she returned to the Hotel on her horse, riding side saddle in her riding habit with bowler hat and net over her face as was the fashion in the thirties. She swept into reception and quite incongruously ordered a pot of china tea and two lightly boiled eggs, which somehow did not fit in with her dress and manner.

Then there was the York family who were keen tennis players and allegedly had their own red shale tennis court built by manufacturers "En Tout Cas". They were said to play tennis at every opportunity.

There was a Scottish lady called Miss Lucy Crockett. She had twinkling eyes and was known to the Gunn children who played at the Hotel as Aunty Lucy.

Living at the top of the Hotel in the twenties was a former World War One soldier who had been gassed in the War. He was rather eccentric and did not mix with the other residents. From time to time he went to Manchester on holiday and under-porter Albert Eaton had to bring his large sea-trunk down on the luggage lift, heave it onto a handcart and push it all the way to Nantwich Railway Station. It was very heavy work and on return from Manchester the soldier used to ring the Hotel and poor Albert had to lug the sea-trunk back again.

Perhaps the most unusual guest at the Hotel, who was semi-permanent, was an Armenian gentleman by the name of Mr Afoumado. He stayed at the Hotel for six months every year where he plied his trade, selling expensive carpets, from the ballroom. It was said that the Hotel was completely carpeted with Mr Afoumado's carpets, which were of a superior quality, all hand made. Mr Afoumado said he could tell by looking at one of his carpets which family had made it. The other six months of the year he sold his carpets from a Hotel in the West End of London. The Gunn children recall how he used to chase them out of the ballroom when they went there to play. He was obviously on very good terms with Mr Worsey and attended his funeral in 1932.

On average during these years between the wars there was up to a maximum of thirty permanent residents at the Hotel. The original square entrance hall to the Hotel was quite small and entered through double doors that were glazed three-quarters of the way down. On the left an enormous high-backed settle jutted out at right angles from the wall completely hiding the large stone fireplace and seating opposite. All the guests knew each other and it was like a large country house party. The permanent residents used to gather here around the fireplace completely hidden from the casual visitor. They were able to watch, unseen by others, the comings and goings of people to and from the Hotel.

... Three months after Mr Worsey's death, Henry Manley and Son, Auctioneers of Crewe, held a sale at the Hotel on 8th December 1932 when the Hotel, together with 72 acres of land including the Brine Baths Farm and 4 cottages were put up for sale.

It was bought by a company called Mackie and Gladstone. The Gladstone part of the partnership related to the Gladstone family of Hawarden Castle. Following this sale, Henry Manley and Son again returned to the Hotel on 28th February 1933 when a large 5 day sale was held to dispose of the many works of art and antiques which covered almost all of the available wall space in the Hotel. It is remarkable that even after this sale there were still sufficient works of art to furnish the Hotel to a high standard.'

The hotel never quite recovered to its earlier heyday and gradual decline set in over the ensuing years. In 1942, it was taken over by the Ministry of Defence and the army moved in, with training taking place in the grounds and also at Parkfield. In 1943, the army moved out and it was then used as accommodation for WAAF personnel who were working at the nearby RAF camp at Hack Green. At the end of the war, the Ministry of Defence pulled out and the Hotel tried to resume its former role but without success.

The hotel closed in 1947 and it was sold to the Club Union who converted it into a convalescent home for miners in 1948. It remained open for four years until 1952 when it closed down and the Club Union put it up for sale. Unable to find a buyer, the hotel was eventually demolished in 1959 and now a large housing estate stands where the hotel and grounds used to be. The line of Western Avenue follows the route of the old service road to the rear of the hotel and Orchard Crescent follows exactly the line of the wall that surrounded the old walled garden.

6. Brine House

There is scant information regarding this property. It is thought to have been built at the same time as Redsands Children's Home at Willaston around 1972, and it used to stand where Brook Way now is.

It was built to house problem children from the local area and run by the County Council Social Services. As it was situated on a housing estate and very close to other houses there were constant complaints from the local residents. The house closed in 1994 after years of campaigning by residents fed up with youngsters causing a disturbance. Their protests reached a peak the year before when teenagers staged a rooftop riot, hurling missiles at police and it shocked onlookers. The building was demolished soon after, and now 11 houses and gardens occupy the same site in Brook Way. There is no trace of the previous building.

12 Marsh Lane, Millfields

1. Marsh Bank Mill

There is a reference in an article printed in *Cheshire History*, Nos. 10 to16 entitled Cornmill Sites in Cheshire 1086–1850 by Oliver Bott. This, with a grid reference, mentions a cornmill, possibly water-powered, on the east (sic) side of Marsh Lane, Nantwich. The building was probably C19.

A building still exists on this site but is much altered. No written records survive to substantiate the claim of a cornmill. There is a Mr Cheatham, miller, listed as living at No.3 Marsh Lane, on the opposite side of the road in 1896.

2. Overleigh, 33 Marsh Lane

A large attractive house, set back from the road in substantial gardens, stood here until some two years ago (2003). It was lived in by the family of Frank Holland, well-known cheese factor, from 1949 to 1990. It was then sold to Dr Davenport whose practice is in Wrenbury. Amid much controversy and opposition from local residents living nearby, the site was sold to developers, the house demolished and three new houses built there.

Miranda Howle (née Holland) wrote to the *Nantwich Chronicle* some time around 2001, saying that she was appalled that the house was being demolished:

> 'It was once a lovely house on the outskirts of a charming historic town. It is now a town house, a little gem surrounded by established trees, lawns and gardens... It may not be in a conservation area but when my father, Frank Holland, was alive people would stop us in the town to tell us how much pleasure it gave them to pass by the garden. Surely we must treasure a little green oasis? Perhaps it is time to start conserving for the sake of future generations... It is not a listed building but it is an attractive solidly built pre-war house. It was once considered to be one of the nicest houses in Nantwich. I no longer live in Nantwich but I am saddened to see the town's unique individuality being eroded.'

Alas, the protestations were of no avail and demolition proceeded.

3. Shenton's Cottage

There are postcards, a photograph and drawing of a black and white cottage which is known to have been at one time in Marsh Lane. The only clue to its whereabouts was the words Shenton's cottage written on the back of one postcard. Both directories of 1896 and 1913 list John Shenton, shoemaker as living at No.24 Marsh Lane which would tie in with the position of the house on early maps. This cottage actually stood where Marsh Bank House is now, the present No.24 Marsh Lane being later built much nearer Welsh Row.

Assuming that the above deduction is correct, then the 1792 Rate Books show that Mr

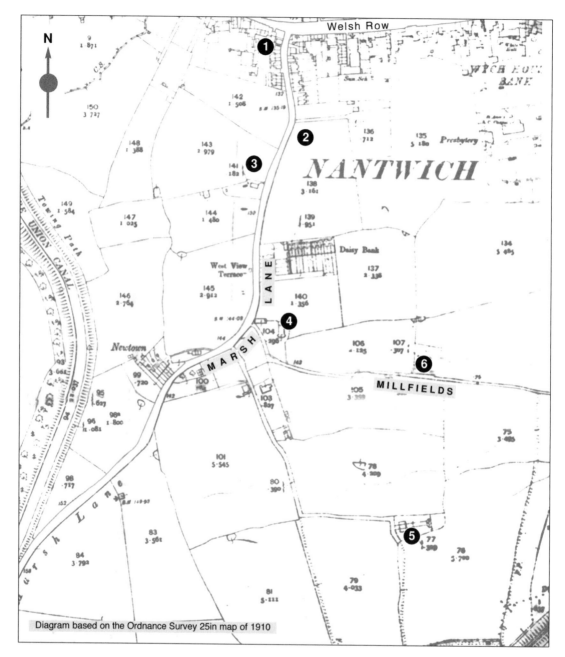

Diagram based on the Ordnance Survey 25in map of 1910

Marsh Lane, Millfields

1 Marsh Bank Mill
2 Overleigh, 33 Marsh Lane
3 Shenton s Cottage
4 The Cedars, 65 Marsh Lane
5 Cottages in Copes Lane
6 Cottages in Millfields

Above: Overleigh 33 Marsh Lane. A fine post-war house demolished and replaced by three modern houses.

The Old Cottage of Marsh Lane Nantwich.

Herbert St John Jones 1914.

Above: Shenton's cottage. An old black and white cottage in Marsh Lane thought to have been on the site of Marsh Bank House.

Above: The Cedars 65 Marsh Lane. The East wall showing the original front door. This building, although still standing is due for demolition at the time of writing. It was called variously Newton and Newtown Cottage after the immediate area which used to be known as Newtown.

Above: West and South elevation of the Cedars.

Left: East and North facing view of the Cedars.

Watkis owned the property and that it may have been two cottages, both described as house and garden. John Hassall lived in one and in the other, Daniel Walley. In 1833 there was no-one in the first cottage and Mr Jeffries lived in the other. Around 1880 it was owned by the Downes family (who also lived at No. 50, Welsh Row) and the occupier was Elizabeth Beckett. The black and white cottage was obviously demolished some time after 1913.

4. The Cedars, 65 Marsh Lane

Although still standing at the time of writing (2005) this building is considered important enough to be included, although due for demolition shortly. In 1792 it was described as house and garden and owned by William Watkis (an attorney who then lived at No.50 Welsh Row) and occupied by William Fleming. In 1833 it was occupied by Widow Burrows.

It was called either Newton Cottage or Newtown Cottage in the mid to late 1800s, the area in the immediate vicinity in Marsh Lane being known at that time, and earlier, as Newtown.

In 1847 it is described as cottage, garden etc., owned by Sampson Cartwright Senior, miller, baker and confectioner who also built Willaston Cottage and owned Taylor's Mill in Crewe Road. It is quite possible that he also had Newtown Cottage built. The occupier in that year was Elizabeth Buckley.

In 1850 Samuel Chorlton, solicitor lived here. In 1869 it was Mrs Susan Whalley here and in 1874 Mrs Sarah Whalley. In 1896 it was Miss Whalley and in 1914, James Cope of the family who lived at Fields Farm, Edleston and owned much of the surrounding area. Cope's Lane is very close to the above property.

By 1928 James Cope must have died as the owner/occupier was his widow, Mary Cope. She sold the house and five acres to Mr Dutton, a local builder and he apparently built the houses in Cherry Grove and some at the top end of Millfields. In 1960 Ivan Hoffe was the owner who then sold the house in 1972 to Mr P Murphy in whose possession it still is.

5. Cottages in Cope's Lane

The 1875 OS Edition Map indicates that there were three cottages situated about half-way down Cope's Lane towards Fields Farm, Edleston. There is no information to be found regarding who lived there. They were demolished some time afterwards, and the housing estate around Gerard Drive now stands somewhere on this site.

6. Cottages in Millfields

The 1910 OS 3rd Edition Map shows two cottages in Millfields standing somewhere where Mill House in Millfields is now. There is no information regarding who lived here, or when they were demolished.

7. Primitive Methodist Chapel, Marsh Lane

Hall mentions a chapel in Marsh Lane, whereabouts unknown.

'Foremost among the leading members of the infant society were Thomas Bateman, of Chorley, and Mr Taylor, who, on 1st Aug.1826, purchased on their own responsibility, (for the society was then as poor as it was small) a building in Marsh Lane for £100, and fitted it with seats, gallery and pulpit, and there this new sect of nonconformists, known then by the name of *Ranters*, worshipped until the year 1840; when, mainly, through the exertions and perseverance of Mr Bateman, (Mr Taylor having died in 1837) the present Chapel was built in Welsh Row, and opened on the 21st October in that year.'

BIBLIOGRAPHY

Cheshire Trade Directories, 1789 onwards

Dabbers Dissenting, 2003

Dodgson J, McN, *The Placenames of Cheshire*, Pt.3: Nantwich Hundred, 1971

Garton E, *Saxon to Puritan*, 1972

Hall J, *The History of Nantwich*, 1883

Hoole WH, *The Cricketing Squire*, 1991

Horner P, *The Life of Charles Laxton, High Constable of Police, Nantwich*, 2003

Hughes D, *The Brine Baths Hotel, Nantwich*, 1994

Johnson's Almanacs 1933 onwards

King D, *Vale Royal* 1656

Lee W, *Report to the General Board of Health*, Nantwich, 1850

Lloyd E, *Nantwich and Acton Grammar School*, 1960

MacGregor Dr AJ, *The Inns and Innkeepers of Nantwich*, 1992

McNeil Sale R, *The Crown Car Park Excavations*, 1978

Mills Mrs I, *Threads in the Life of John Mills*

Nantwich Chronicle

Nantwich Civic Society Newsletters

Nantwich Town Rate Books, 1691 onwards

Partridge The Rev. J, *The History of Nantwich*, 1774

Richards R, *Old Cheshire Churches*, 2nd Ed., 1972

Simpson S, *Within Living Memory*, 1990

Vaughan D, *Nantwich, it was like this*, 1987

Wall P, The Life and Times of a Great Victorian Sporting Hero, AN Hornby, (unpub.)

INDEX